Who the Hell is
Müller-Brockmann?

T0277880

Who the Hell is Müller-Brockmann?

Conversations about the Swiss Style

Demian Conrad

Just as in nature systems of order govern the growth
and structure of animate and inanimate matter,
so human activity itself has, since the earliest times,
been distinguished by the quest for order.

— Josef Müller-Brockmann

Contents

When I joined the Culture Department at the Embassy of Switzerland in London, I inherited an office with hundreds of art books from a long line of cultural attachés, accumulated over decades. One of my first tasks was to go through all the publications, some of which dated back to the 1970s, catalogue them and discard what was no longer relevant for our work in the 21st century. We organised a large Swiss art book giveaway and many publications found new homes with artists and designers in our wider network. However, there was a stack of unassuming looking publications that I was instructed to hold on to for as long as possible, as we would have regular requests from academics desperately looking for these rare books. One of them, a musty, yellowing paperback sitting at the back of my shelves, was Jost Hochuli's *Book Design in Switzerland*, published in 1993 by the Swiss Arts Council, Pro Helvetia. To this day, it is considered a reference work amongst graphic designers and typographers, and, since it has been out of print for more than two decades, it sells for substantial sums on digital platforms such as eBay.

My second surprise was when the Swiss-British graphic design studio Kellenberger White organised a panel conversation about the Federal Book Design Prize, The Most Beautiful Swiss Books, which was so oversubscribed that people had to be turned away at the door. Swiss graphic design has been conquering the world ever since the 1950s. Whilst it is definitely the subtlest, it was probably also the most radical, innovative and influential export the country ever had. Generations of typographers and graphic designers have since adopted and developed the minimal, clean Swiss style, spreading it across the globe. However, I was intrigued that British and international audiences continued to show such an appetite for contemporary Swiss graphic design. Institutions such as HEAD – Genève (Haute École d'Art et de Design), écal (École Cantonale d'Art de Lausanne) and ZHdK (Zurich University of the Arts), amongst many others, continue to break boundaries and remain authorities in the field. Whereas recent generations have moved on from the rigidity of the *Grid Systems* established during the early days of the movement, the tradition of conveying a message through the art of type lives on. In addition, there is also a sensitivity amongst the broader public that, when it comes to identity, from small businesses to large corporate entities, a designer needs to be involved. Switzerland is design.

When the Culture Department was offered a project space at the creative agency Blattler Ltd. on 53 Fashion Street in London, it was clear that graphic design and type would be a major factor in the programming of the series of design exhibitions. The series, entitled *Ambit*, meaning the scope, extent, or bounds of something, explored, over the course of about thirty small exhibitions over three years, the range of what Swiss design encompasses, from Maximage's *Color Library* to a micro-retrospective of Jost Hochuli's body of work. In 2017, in a conversation with Demian Conrad, his project *Who the Hell is Müller-Brockmann?* began to take shape. We were thrilled to welcome him into our programme, not just to have him present UK audiences with recent Swiss design, but also because of this investigation into the profound resonance Swiss design has had among designers in the UK and how it has been reflected in their work. Demian's week-long residency enabled him to meet many London-based designers in a small space and interview them about their design journeys and influences. The result was a kaleidoscopic collage of design references that covered the walls of the gallery. We are delighted that some years down the road, this selection of those conversations has been assembled in this publication, presenting a snapshot of Swiss design's reverberations among contemporary designers – a conversation that is in flux, and will continue.

David Kilian Beck

Head of Culture
Embassy of Switzerland in the United Kingdom

I made my first trip to London in 1995. I was on a field trip from my school to visit the most innovative studios of the time. Our stops included the preeminent Pentagram, the brand new but up-and-coming Graphic Through Facilities, North Design (who were just finishing up their visual identity for RAC Limited), Boom Design (a company working on websites that went bust), and the legendary Dennis Bailey. It was an inspirational point in my life, being able to step into these renowned studios, and gaze upon walls that reflected so many original ideas, and I savoured the cosmopolitan ambiance of London.

The main event was our visit to the co-founder of Pentagram, the eminent Alan Fletcher, who, as of 1992, had launched his career as an independent designer. The visit had been planned for the end of the day, and, since it was winter, night had already fallen. Fletcher's home was in the chic neighbourhood of Notting Hill. The magnificent whiteness of the façades and the bright lights were dazzling and somehow frightening at the same time. Fletcher lived in a house tucked into a mews. The inside court-yard was wonderful: the ground was paved with red brick and traditional English ivy wound its way over the walls of the houses. When we reached the entrance to the house, we paused before a large iron gate forged into all the letters of the alphabet in an ultra-condensed type. It wasn't easily legible but the message was clear: here resides a graphic designer. We rang and a rather thickset man descended the stairs and came to open the door. Fletcher gave the impression of a very serious man, but as one got to know him over time, you discovered that beneath that exterior lay the soul of a child, and his eyes always betrayed an inner playfulness. In his vast studio, everything was white and minimalistic, the only hints of colour were his works in primary colours arranged in a structured and meticulous manner along the walls; they appeared to have been positioned according to the *Grid Systems*. Several tables were littered with a series of beer mugs in grey ceramic; a little smile, drawn by hand with a simple black line, decorated each one. The visual trick was that, when two mugs came together for a toast, the faces gave the impression they were kissing. The project had been commissioned by the Office of Tourism of Munich to celebrate Oktoberfest. He went on to recount a series of anecdotes about the various projects he was working on. I only remember one: at the end of the presentation, I asked him about his relationship with technology. For those of us who were graduates in 1997, the advent of the computer was seen as the birth of a creative tool that would change the world. His consistently serious face lit up with a little smile. He invited us over to the other side of the room where a Swiss army surplus blanket, with its iconic white cross on a red background, was draped over a Macintosh. He stood next to the desk, gestured towards it and said: 'Here lies, hidden beneath this cloak furnished by the Swiss army, my Macintosh, which I only use in case of emergency.' His comment was amusing, but also laden with nuance. Seeing this Swiss object in the atelier of this great master had intrigued me a great deal.

The story of this book begins in 2016, when I discovered that David Kilian Beck, who is now Head of Culture at the Swiss embassy in London, possessed one of my posters, *The Golden Dot*, which I had designed that same year for the referendum vote on unconditional basic income. He subsequently invited me to participate in his cultural programme in October of 2017 at the Ambit Gallery, a small space in

Detail shot of the collage installation made up of A4 photocopies made over the course of Conrad's week-long residency.

Flyer for the residency and installation at the Ambit Gallery in Brick Lane. It was designed by Automatico Studio, using a blend of Helvetica and Gill Sans typefaces.

the vibrant multicultural quarter of Brick Lane. Since the project was sponsored by the embassy, I wanted to examine the question of cultural exchanges, exploring not only travels but relationships between ideas, and knowledge shared. My idea was to spend five days at the gallery in a sort of residency, and invite as many people as possible to come participate and share their anecdotes and stories about the influence of Swiss design in Britain and vice versa. The selection of interviewees was a sort of natural selection over the course of a week. I remember Richard Hollis arriving at the gallery with a little wooden cane in one hand and an old photocopied map of the area in the other. Several major figures whom I contacted could not participate, either due to the time constraints or for personal reasons, notably Ken Garland, who remains a key figure in the relationships created between graphic designers in both countries, also Sean Perkins from North, Eva Kellenberger and Sebastian White of Kellenberger/White, and Catherine Dixon, among others.

Our working space within the showcase space consisted of a white table, a chair made by a Swiss company, another chair made by a British company, a black-and-white photocopier, a recorder with microphone, and, of course, a bit of Swiss chocolate and Swiss coffee. Each participant was asked to bring a Swiss object that had profoundly influenced them to touch off the discussions. Over the course of the week, many magnificent objects went in and out of that space: an original letter, written by Emil Ruder, a book dedication written by Josef Müller-Brockmann (JMB), as well as original editions of JMB's manual, which appeared three times, along with a first edition of Karl Gerstner's *Designing Programmes*. When the interviewees arrived at the gallery,

The setting of the installation: the wall featuring photocopies of the participant's objects, a white table, a Swiss chair by Vitra and a British chair by Another Country.

Holger Jacobs and Demian Conrad in discussion over British coffee and Swiss chocolate, with tools of graphic design on the table.

I offered them a coffee, then we sat down to chat. Each interview lasted around an hour. Then their object was photocopied, as a testament to the discussion, and hung on the gallery wall as part of a growing mosaic of images and memories. Day by day, the mosaic grew and the wall was covered with additional images that lent a more personal perspective. At the end of the week, the wall was entirely covered, and the result was left up on display for the rest of the month. Travel emerges as one of the key themes of this work, as seen by the objects brought by Hollis, such as Swiss railway brochures from the 1930s and 1940s, Swissair publications, or the anecdotes of Sara De Bondt.

The collaboration with Niggli is an important one, since they were central to the international diffusion of Müller-Brockmann's writings, such as *Grid Systems* or *The Graphic Artist and His Design Problems*, along with other seminal works. This book does not have scientific pretensions, it is rather an informal exploration by a practitioner of design who is interested in the aesthetics of relationships and personal stories, a sort of personal tribute as a graphic designer. For this work, I opted to focus most specifically upon graphic design and consequently selected eight interviews out of the fifteen I originally conducted. It was not an easy task but one that allowed me to fulfil my initial intent. I would like to extend a special thanks to Freda Sack, who left us in 2019. Freda was a woman of great intelligence and humanity. It was she who made it possible for Müller-Brockmann to come to London in 1996, inviting him to lecture at the International Society of Typographic Designers (ISTD).

Undoubtedly, the 2016 exhibition *Les Suisses de Paris* at the Museum für Gestaltung in Zurich was a source of inspiration for *Who the Hell is Müller-Brockmann?* The impact made by Swiss graphic design in London is obvious, but the influence was felt in both directions. Some notable examples are Fletcher's long collaboration with Novartis as their creative director, the creation of the identity for Swiss International Airlines by Winkreative, as well as many other stories contained in this work. I hope that this product of my journey will spark your curiosity and hopefully encourage you to further explore this subject. *Buona lettura! Viel Spass beim lesen!* Happy reading!

Demian Conrad

A few years ago, one of my clients, a smart and visually astute individual, commissioned me to design a book. When I showed him some early page layouts, he said: 'Very nice. Very Müller-Brockmann'. This surprised me. I didn't expect him to know who Josef Müller-Brockmann was. And although the design didn't borrow directly from JMB, my client wasn't entirely mistaken either. The layouts owed a debt to mid-century Swiss modernist design. They adhered to a modular grid. There was a generous helping of white space. The text was set in a sans-serif typeface and the pages had an unadorned clarity that was as recognisably Swiss as a block of *Emmentaler*.

My client's comment alerted me to something I hadn't grasped before: Müller-Brockmann had now become a designation for a stylistic and conceptual school of design. In his case, a national school of design – Swiss modernist design. Very few graphic designers achieve this status, perhaps only a tiny number throughout history. But it's clear that JMB was one of this select band. He didn't invent Swiss modernist design, but in the eyes of many, he was its most notable practitioner. His name and Swiss design have become synonymous. Who else can say that the mere mention of their name immediately defines a body of graphic expression? To get an answer to this question, I posted the following on Twitter:

> 'I'm writing about how graphic designers represent schools, style or genre of graphic expression. Clearly, it's the designers who have followers who perpetuate the stylistic voice. I'd say Josef Müller-Brockmann was one. Who else?'

The responses were varied and for the most part, predictable. Frequently mentioned names included Wim Crouwel, Saul Bass, Wolfgang Weingart, Grapus, David Carson, Neville Brody, Vaughan Oliver, Metahaven. Disappointingly, apart from one Japanese recommendation (Yusaku Kamekura), there were no suggestions from outside the Euro-American graphic design enclave.

All the designers mentioned are undeniably influential and have dedicated followers, but can any of them be said to represent an entire genre of visual design, at least to the same degree that it can be said of Müller-Brockmann? Wim Crouwel represents a wing of 20th century Dutch design, but by no means the whole of Dutch design. David Carson inspired a generation of young designers, but his influence, though extensive, was short-lived. Metahaven have been influential amongst adventurous British design students, inspiring many copyists, but will this influence still be with us in ten years' time?

What happens if we add a supplementary question: how many of the above mentioned names could be said to have a recognition factor that extends beyond professional graphic design? Thanks to his standing in the film world, we would probably include Saul Bass, and perhaps Vaughan Oliver, whose work has a high recognition factor within the music world. Furthermore, although we can add Müller-Brockmann's name to this list, it's doubtful if any of the others mentioned above have forged a style that is widely recognised by non-designers. Swiss design experts will – rightly – point out that JMB was as much a product of Swiss design philosophy as he was one of its co-creators. His early work from the 1940s and 1950s – twee illustrations and whimsical layouts – was about as far as it's possible to get from high Swiss modernism. Nevertheless, together with a cohort of influential figures – Max Bill, Armin Hoffman, Emil Ruder, Richard Paul Lohse, among others – JMB was one of the designers responsible for devising, promulgating, and exporting the Swiss style.

In today's culture we have learned to be wary of using national boundaries as the sole defining quality of identity. Countries are not discrete entities – they are physical locations defined by their complex histories, by their neighbours, and in many cases, by patterns of immigration and emigration. Switzerland is a case in point. A landlocked country with three official languages, it owes an existential debt to its powerful neighbours, France, Germany and Italy. In graphic design terms, we only have to think of the role played by German-born Jan Tschichold, who came to Switzerland to advance his ideas around modern typography, ideas that greatly influenced the indigenous Swiss modernists. Yet while recognising the complexity and indeterminacy of national identity, most graphic designers understand what is meant by the term Swiss design or Swiss style, and, for most designers, Josef Müller-Brockmann is as good a representative of that understanding as any.

For me, and many of my generation, the infatuation with JMB began in the 1990s. This can be largely attributed to the publication of his book *Pioneer of Swiss Graphic Design* (1966). As both the writer and publisher, Lars Müller was responsible for making a seismic impact on British designers. The book's impact can be likened to Brian Eno's famous and slightly hyperbolic observation about the Velvet Underground's first album (*The Velvet Underground & Nico,* 1966): not many people bought it, Eno said, but everyone who did, formed a band. Lars Müller's tome did not achieve airport blockbuster sales levels, but for a design book it sold healthily and everyone who bought a copy either started a design studio or dreamt of doing so.

What did the 1990s generation of designers see in Müller-Brockmann's work? They saw a new way of making work that opposed the hegemony of ideas-led graphic design – the dominant school of British graphic expression in the 1970s and 1980s. This mode of graphic expression relied on visual puns, metaphoric images and what its practitioners liked to call 'graphic wit'. It became known as the 'Smile in the Mind' school of design. A book with the same title, published in 1996, became the movement's bible.

As a young designer I saw a piece of work that captured this conceptual approach: its discovery prompted a minor epiphany. The cover of the published sheet music for the musical *Singin' in the Rain* featured a music manuscript with bars, notes and staves. It had been splashed with droplets of water, thus creating the impression that the manuscript had been left out in the rain. I could see that the idea had a clever immediacy, but I found its obviousness off-putting. Like a joke often retold, it soon became wearing, and it impressed my young mind with the conviction that I didn't want to work in that way. Modernist Swiss design offered a radical alternative to *Smile in the Mind* graphics. And yet it is one of the ironies of Swiss design that, despite its reliance on logic and reverence for industrial standardisation and scientific notions of rationality, its most potent formative influence came from modern art. It owed a foundational debt to Cubism (the elimination of perspective – everything on the same plane); Constructivism (the use of geometric forms and the primacy of 'factual' photography over 'imprecise' illustration), and to Concrete Art (a movement that stipulated that work should refer to nothing other than itself). Max Bill spelt this out as far back as 1936 when he wrote:

> Concrete design is design that emerges from its own resources and rules, without having to derive or borrow these from external natural phenomena. Visual design is thus based on colour, form, space, light, movement.[1]

Bill goes on to liken this new conception of visual design to music, in which sound is not based on an 'imitation of nature'. In Bill's conception, by following the example of music, a new visual autonomy entered graphic communication – form could just be form; space could just be space; typography was no longer dependent on humanist, metaphorical or ornamental traditions. This freedom was grasped by a generation of British designers, most of whom had emerged from art schools during the 1980s. Design groups such as Farrow, North, and Cartlidge Levene produced graphic design that was infused with Swiss aesthetic principles. It was deployed as a multipurpose style in precisely the way that its founders had envisaged. It appeared on album covers and in property brochures. For many designers, it was an invigorating break from the insularity of British graphic design and a reflection of a new and growing sense of 'Europeanness'.

For Michael C. Place, a highly individualistic UK designer, his introduction to JMB came in the early 2000s, making him, as he notes, 'a latecomer!' Yet, while he was enthralled with JMB's work, it did not turn him into a copyist, instead it acted as a springboard for developing his own design philosophy:

> My introduction to Swiss style was more from the Swiss-Punk end rather than the purists' view. But at an exhibition I attended, I was particularly drawn to the beautiful sense of movement in JMB's posters for *Musica Viva* (Zurich Tonhalle). I think the big takeaway for me was a sense of space and scale. But it also taught me that it's not the only way to design, and instead to

[1] As cited in Müller, Lars, *Josef Müller-Brockmann,*
Pioneer of Swiss Graphic Design, (Lars Müller, 2015) page 14–15.
[2] From an interview between Adrian Shaughnessy and Michael C. Place.

take the influence and bend and distort it to your own will. To be brave. For me purism isn't what is exciting about graphic design, I admire it but it's not what interests me.[2]

Nevertheless, JMB left an enduring impression on Place; he was sufficiently inspired to name his two Sphynx cats Müller and Brockmann.

Yet, Britain in the 1990s and early 2000s was not Switzerland in the 1960s. Designers were functioning in an ever-toughening commercial environment that demanded impact and drama. Swiss style might work for Pet Shop Boys' album covers, but mainstream clients wanted something more; they wanted potency and many of them saw the updated Swiss modernist style as airless and lacking in emotion. Design critics were also unimpressed. Some saw it as an example of the theft of a style without an understanding of the cultural and conceptual principles behind the work – what today, in these decolonising times, we would describe as 'cultural appropriation'. The British designers who adopted the Swiss style in the 1990s were not the first to do so. The arrival in the UK of the magazines *Graphis* (1944) and *Neue Grafik* (1958), of which JMB was a co-founder and co-editor, and from a slightly later period, JMB's book, *The Graphic Artist and His Design Problems* (1961), galvanised a small group of British designers who had latched onto this revolutionary way of creating visual communication. Richard Hollis, Ken Garland, Anthony Froshaug and Dennis Bailey all travelled to Switzerland at the end of the 1950s. They came back enthralled with what they saw and set about introducing their discoveries into British design. Traditionally resistant to the ideas of modernism, a new rigour and clarity was smuggled into the way British institutions, products and services presented themselves. Identities and house styles for Penguin, Galt Toys, British Rail, British Steel, and the National Theatre demonstrated an alternative to what the émigré designer FHK Henrion called design by 'crayon and airbrush'.

In his study of the impact of Swiss design on British designers, *Swiss Graphic Design: A British Invention?*, design historian Robert Lzicar explores the way British graphic designers adopted – and adapted – Swiss designtheory and practice. He identifies three ways in which Swiss style was absorbed into the unlikely terrain of British visual design:

'…on several levels of the discourse, British actors contributed both to the construction of Swiss graphic design and to our current understanding of it. First, British graphic designers reported on graphic design from Switzerland and thus disseminated their experiences and their interpretation of that design in and according to the British design discourse. Second, graphic designers incorporated the stylistic characteristics and methods of *Konstruktive Gebrauchsgrafik* in their design of objects and thus into British visual culture. And third, practitioner-historians contributed in retrospect to the construction of the labels 'Swiss graphic design' and 'Swiss typography' to signify an epoch of graphic design history.'[3]

Besides the high modernism espoused by JMB and others, different strands of Swiss design found their way into the British graphic design vocabulary. In the 1980s Neville Brody moved away from his much-copied constructivist style and used Helvetica in his design and art direction for *Arena* magazine. Brody's use of this quintessential Swiss typeface was far more buoyant and painterly than the way it was used in Switzerland, but it demonstrated how the unapologetic use of sans-serif typography could be as effective as more ostentatious typographic strategies. The work of Zurich-based Odermatt & Tissi (Siegfried Odermatt and Rosmarie Tissi) offered a playful and less rigid take on the work of the Swiss arch-modernists. Wolfgang Weingart's postmodernist constructions inspired a loyal following amongst young British graphic designers. They took inspiration from Weingart's belief in the melding of self-expression with typographic rigour, albeit typography of a more flamboyant kind than that practiced by his compatriot predecessors. Hamish Muir, one of the founders of 8vo, studied under Weingart in Basel, and brought his thinking to the group's celebrated self-produced publication *Octavo* – the *Neue Grafik* of its time. April Greiman also studied under Weingart and took his ideas back to the USA where she helped spark the American New Wave movement of the 1980s and 1990s – a movement facilitated by the arrival of the computer, which made Weingart's fluid and mobile layouts readily achievable. Today, Swiss style is just one of numberless stylistic overcoats that British designers put on, or take off, as they please. Plurality rules in modern visual communication – from the free-form to the ultra-structured, anything goes. And although designers are free to raid the dressing-up box of visual styles and codes, the ghost of high Swiss modernism still lingers in the creative palette of British

[3] Lzicar, Robert, 'Swiss Graphic Design: A British Invention?', *Pesign Issues* 2021, 37 (1): 51–63.

graphic design – especially its key tenet, that graphic design now has the freedom to refer to nothing but itself. Although frequently dismissed as a secondary art form, it can be countered that graphic design has now reached a point where, like fine art, it can exist as a discrete discipline with its own traditions, its own philosophy, its own critical framework, its own academic independence, and increasingly its own literature. Although most graphic designers are dependent on clients to provide messages, content and funding, there is also a graphic design that is unmoored from the conventional client/designer dependency. Graphic designers routinely make their own publications and sell their own typefaces. They are active in self-directed social, political and cultural enterprises of all kinds. They even commit the great professional sin of making work purely for their own delight, as well as others. In this they are greatly helped by the rise of social media, which allows designers to publish for a vast audience of appreciative design watchers. Dismissed by some as a betrayal of the professional remit of graphic designers to offer a service, and criticised by others as the production of worthless eye-candy, this relentless experimentation is one of the ways in which new modes of expression are being discovered.

This new-found autonomy was at least partly derived from the Swiss pioneers. JMB and the others who followed him – everyone from Weingart to Norm, from Karl Gerstner to Windlin – showed how it was possible for designers to function as professionals even as they developed their own projects. As Orson Welles's character said in the film *The Third Man*: 'In Switzerland, they had brotherly love, they had five hundred years of democracy and peace. And what did that produce? The cuckoo clock'. Welles was wrong. Cuckoo clocks came from Germany. However, if he had said graphic design instead of cuckoo clocks, he would have been right.

Adrian Shaughnessy

Inside of the Demian Conrad's one week residence
at Ambit Gallery in Bricklane, London, 2017

BIR

& Marketing

Mob : 07984 116 196

53a

umlaut"

am[ ]bit

Who t

WHO
THE
HELL
IS
MR
BROCK-
MANN?

WHO
THE
HELL
IS
MR
BROCK-
MANN?

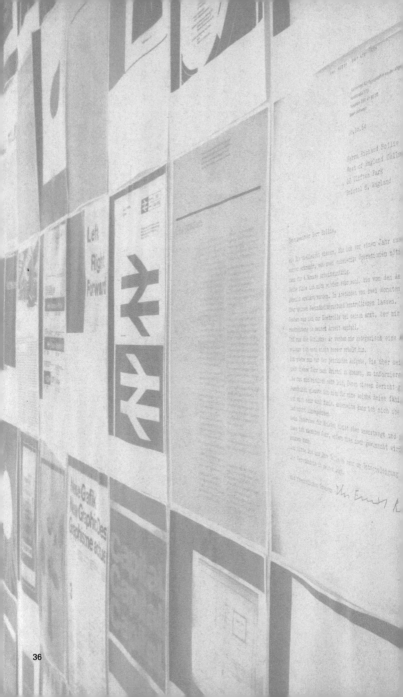

a

Bruno Maag

DEMIAN CONRAD: Last time we met was in Lugano (Ticino) for a talk about typography. I was impressed by the scope of your design for the Nokia font. I'm curious about the object you have brought here to start our discussion.

BRUNO MAAG: I have brought two pictures. One is a picture of a file (page 50) and one is a picture of a line: (page 51) they don't seem very spectacular but each one symbolises something very personal, and they are what sparked my getting into typography. It goes all the way back to when I was sixteen years old. As you know, in Switzerland, even today we still do traditional apprenticeships. I was coming to the end of secondary school and like everyone else, I was wondering what I was going to do for the rest of my life. I thought, 'OK, I've got to find an apprenticeship and learn a skill.' I was born in Zurich and all the men in my family were mechanical engineers: my dad, my granddad, my great granddad, my great uncle. So, logic would follow that I should become a mechanical engineer. It was 1978, and there was a bit of a recession going on, but eventually I acquired some work experience at a company which at the time was probably the top engineering company in the world. They specialised in building machines for making tools. Anyway, this is where the file comes in... I was starting this week-long internship, beginning at 7:00 AM on a miserable February morning. I walk into this factory, into a hall the size of a football pitch. There are about 300 people in there and everyone is filing away at some piece of metal... and I'm thinking 'Fuck me! God strike me down if I have to do this for the rest of my life! I want to die now!' It literally was like that! I walked in there and I knew I was not going to do that.

I took an instant dislike to it. Still, I did finish up the week obviously, since I had made a commitment, but at the end the supervisor came over and said, 'Don't even think of applying for a job! You are not meant to be here!' I just said, 'Thank you, I wasn't going to!' So I went back home, and had a chat with my parents. They understood that I didn't like the work, so my mum said, 'What about the printing industry?' It just so happened that my dad had worked for a little while at a newspaper as an engineer, maintaining the printing machines. He said, 'I know a couple of people, let me get in touch with them.' As a result, I secured an apprenticeship as a typesetter, or *Schriftsetzer* with the newspaper *Tages-Anzeiger*. So, once again, there I was at 7:00 AM on a Monday morning, walking into their print shop, but this time the thought that flashed through my mind was, 'This is what I'm going to do for the rest of my life.' I knew it, there and then. This is why this picture of the file is so significant, it illustrates those moments of clarity, when I stepped into a place of work and immediately knew whether it was right for me, or not. I completed a four-year apprenticeship: for the first three years, I was mainly hand typesetting. I also received a brief introduction to Monotype and Linotype machine setting, and of course letterpress and offset printing, since understanding production processes is an important part of the job. I was also extremely lucky because being at the *Tages-Anzeiger* was probably the best apprentice-ship one could get. One of the things I remember really well from my first year of apprenticeship was Friday afternoons. I had to clean the proofing presses, which I really didn't like! I also had to collect all the waste paper for recycling. One of my jobs was to take the paper down into the bowels of the building to the collection point, where the big rotation press was also located. This was a task that could have been done in fifteen minutes but I would stretch it out to two hours because at that time of the afternoon, around 3:00 PM, they would start printing the sections of the paper that were not reliant on late news.

The engineers and printers in the print room would begin by feeding the paper through the press very slowly, gradually ramping up the print speed. As the machines approached about 10,000 editions an hour, everyone would be frantically running around tuning dials regulating humidity and temperature. Everything would vibrate: printing a newspaper was a very visceral experience. Then, all of a sudden, you would hear a loud bang when the paper ripped and the press would come to a full stop. Everyone would be yelling and swearing as they had start feeding the paper through the machine once again, which was really tedious. I thought it was all very exciting, and I loved it. I really did. Another thing I loved was that the people working in this industry were eccentric, in a good way. I don't think they would fit in today's society anymore, some could probably be described as mentally unstable. Also another major difference between engineers and typesetters was that engineers would always read the tabloids on their breaks, and typesetters would read the broadsheet [newspapers]. You could have an educated conversation with your colleagues that went beyond the Page Three centerfolds and sports. I would say that education was a job requirement, you had to be highly literate.

DC: It's funny, Richard Hollis, who was just here, mentioned that the British had always been fascinated by the precision of our Swiss print production, to the point of being somewhat jealous.

BM: Yeah, it's a bit like that. I guess the Swiss have always had this thing for precision, and that brings me to my second object: what we have here is just a lower-case letter 'a' – the left side is in Helvetica (page 52), and the right is in Univers (page 53). This brings us to the weird concept of Swiss typography. Today, when you discuss it with young designers they associate it with *Grid Systems* and Helvetica; they think of it as a design style. First of all, I think Swiss typography isn't so much a design style as it is an attitude. The moment you mix Swiss typography and design style, you become dogmatic. Swiss typography is not about dogma. Swiss typography is all about research and finding the best possible solution to a problem. You might say it's a very methodological approach. Whether that approach leads to using a serif type with a lot of ornament, or a sans-serif type that is ultra-minimalistic, is actually quite irrelevant. It is all about the approach. It is all about the attitude. It is about what you do with the problem. I think a lot of people who now evoke Swiss typography are simply applying some sort of dogma but are not practising the attitude. I do believe that invoking Swiss typography today is just being lazy. To be utterly frank, I would say it's a very lazy excuse for just doing the same thing over and over and over again. This is why I increasingly dissociate myself from being described as a Swiss typographer. I also keep repeating to students: 'You are a designer, you are not an artist. If you want to be an artist, you need to fuck off now and go take a different course. Your job is different from that of an artist: it is to analyse and organise information, and present it in an aesthetically pleasing way'. This attitude goes back to when I spent time at the Basel School of Design studying typography and visual communication with Armin Hofmann. On the first day of his class, he reminded us that, as designers, we are problem solvers, ingraining that time and again, like a mantra. Basel was all about methodology, it was about finding the best possible solution to a given problem – whatever that solution might be, and without being dogmatic about it.

I also had Wolfgang Weingart as a teacher for nearly four years. He was fantastic; in my opinion he was the best teacher I ever had. Most people never understood him, but I think he was brilliant. I think he really understood that Swiss typography was all about building and methodology: first you had to build your own skills and then learn the methodology of how to construct solutions for your clients, whatever they may turn out to be.

I remember some work I did toward the end of Weingart's course: a study in composition and colour. It was not Swiss typography in the dogmatic sense but a Swiss typography that was the result of a certain methodology and attitude. The product was 'art' in the widest possible sense, an end result that was the best solution to the problem posed. We now have to talk about Helvetica and Univers. As I mentioned earlier, the notion in people's heads – or rather in young designers' heads who claim to do Swiss typography – is that they have to use Helvetica. However, I would like to challenge that: Helvetica is Swiss and it is undoubtedly an iconic sign of the times. When Helvetica and Univers were first released there was indeed a need for change in the graphic language.

Helvetica and Univers were simply the typographic catalysts for that change. Helvetica is often considered to be modernist, neutral and minimalist but I would argue that it is nothing of the sort. It is Univers, the truly Swiss typeface designed by Adrian Frutiger, that actually possesses all these attributes. Where Helvetica is slapdash, imprecise, almost antique in look and feel, Univers is tight in its precision of tension and strokes. Where Helvetica is irregular in letter spacing, Univers is methodical. I have never understood why people want to use Helvetica for everything. Perhaps it just comes down to laziness, and the safety of thinking they can't go wrong with it. In terms of the history of Helvetica's success, it was first used in American advertising, swiftly establishing itself as the go-to typeface. With the appearance of the Apple Macintosh, Helvetica secured its position by being on every single Mac at the time, further cementing this notion of rational design: Swiss typography. It allowed people to say 'OK, I need to use Swiss typography: here is Helvetica, Helvetica is easy.' So we ended up with bloody Helvetica everywhere. Basically, people think, 'Oh wow, I can just use Helvetica, it's a safe choice that I don't have to justify.' It's a very dogmatic solution and it's being mistaken for Swiss typography. But to me Univers is about as perfect as you can get in terms of typefaces, and it is actually the typeface I would take to a desert island. There is a starkness to it, a calmness: just look at the shape, it amounts to a perfect coming together of an artistic execution of design, in contrast to the laziness of Helvetica. I also quite like Akzidenz-Grotesk: it has that industrial feel to it, with roots going back to 1899, when Queen Victoria still reigned over the British empire. I think it is time to kill the notion that modernism equals Swiss typography in order to move on to a visual language that is fit for the 21st century. I think we need to delete the term Swiss typography from our consciousness in order to free ourselves of design dogmas and make way for design that evolves in keeping with the technologies around it, and, of course, different consumer demands.

DC: I really like your comparison. My *Schriftsetzer* teacher [Meinrad Singenberger] was always referring to these two examples. He also emphasised that Univers was far superior: one's first impression is that it's a bit clinical and cold, but when you get to know it, you discover another world.

BM: I just think, that because of Helvetica's inherent fuzziness – I cannot think of a better word – it's relatively forgiving to use. When you use Univers, you have to be very disciplined. Still, if you use it right, I think you can get so much warmth out of it. It has so much clarity and simplicity, as well as humanity. I think some companies use Univers fairly well: Deutsche Bank uses Univers and I think their application is pretty nice, it doesn't feel impersonal.

I also have no problem with Akzidenz-Grotesk. I find it's actually a very nice typeface. Nonetheless, once again, if you start looking at its history, its roots are in slab serifs. To accommodate small print advertising, *Akzidenzen*, they chopped off the serifs to facilitate small size printing. This is where the name 'grotesk/grotesque' comes from: people were not used to these simplified structures and labelled them 'grotesque'.

DC: Nowadays, it seems that every foundry has to have its own Helvetica typeface product. What do you think of this proliferation of Swiss-like typefaces?

BM: I think it's very much a commercial decision. You need to have a Grotesque-style typeface in your library, because you know they sell. At the end of the day, you have to make money in one way or another, and sometimes having a good Grotesque typeface helps with marketing and gaining traction in the type industry. You may also want to have variations on the theme, with more geometric designs, again very much with an eye on the commercial impact it has on your type business.

DC: Today, if you are doing a bachelor's degree in graphic design, doesn't it seem almost mandatory to design your own typefaces to use in your commercial projects as soon you hit the real world?

BM: Yes. I think it's a good idea because it gives students an appreciation of how difficult it is to design a good typeface. It also provides designers with a bit of a vocabulary – it makes them think about how to communicate, how to speak about type. The downside of that is that a lot of novice designers think that they can design the type for a project and hand it over to the client without considering the implications beyond just the immediate aesthetic. I find sometimes that the design concepts are not properly refined and executed, and the font's engineering is amateurish to the point that the client cannot use it because it is not fit for purpose. It may have fulfilled the immediate creative brief but its implementation for the requirements of a wide body of work were not considered. I also think that design education needs to make it clear that designing a typeface goes beyond a handful of letters, that it is a specialist skill that takes time to refine and hone. This takes us right back to the attitudes associated with Swiss typography. In order to provide the best result for the client, designers must understand methodology.

DC: Let's go back to Britain, since that's also the subject here, as you know. How do you think Swiss typography affected British culture? When you came to London, you brought your Swiss culture, methodology, and your ambitions along with you.

BM: When I first arrived in London, I had come straight from the Basel School of Design and I started working at Monotype. There, everyone, irrespective of their background, whether they had been a baker or a top graphic designer, had to go through a six-week training in drawing. We spent the entire first week practising drawing straight lines, vertical and horizontal (page 51). All day, every day, for eight hours. We would just draw lines, freehand, without a ruler. On Friday afternoon, the supervisor came over and said 'OK, now draw one vertical and one horizontal line over twenty-five centimetres, [ten inches]'. I drew mine and he placed a ruler against them. If I was off by even one millimetre, I would have to practise another week. The second week I did circles. Same thing: every day I drew circles. Friday afternoon, I drew my circle and the supervisor put a compass to it and if I was off by one millimetre, I had to begin practising again! The first two weeks were absolutely soul destroying. I thought, 'I can't do this anymore!' Yet, it was all about the essential rigour of design. That was the methodology: you needed to have the core craftsmanship and skills required to execute your idea. There is another thing I tend to say to both design students and advertisers: your idea might be every bit as good as you think it is – but it all goes to shit if you can't execute it properly. Execution is a vital part of an idea. Concepts are all well and good, but you must be able to execute a concept. Which means you have to have the skills and craftsmanship, or understand that you need another person who has the skills to execute your idea. Of course, in type design, craft is everything. In the days when I started out at Monotype, everyone was still drawing by hand and then the drawings were digitized. Then there was a period of transition around 1989 when people started working directly onscreen using Fontographer. All the discipline I had acquired from my apprenticeship, the Basel School and in Monotype's intro training came in handy because I had acquired the necessary skills for my craft. This Swiss discipline could also be a hindrance; everything works like clockwork in Switzerland, everything is organised. I arrived in London and it all just seemed like chaos, mayhem. It took me about four years to figure out what the British are all about, but in the beginning, I really struggled with it. London life would wind me up every day but after about four or five years I relaxed into it and embraced it. It allowed me to see things another way, from a different perspective. I think this influenced me quite a bit as a designer. I can still apply and instil discipline and rigour but now, I am also much more open to alternative approaches. Culturally, I think that perhaps the Swiss and the British people are not all that different. I think the Swiss are quite reserved, as are the British, although maybe less so in London. London can almost be classified as a different country. Still, if you venture outside London, you find that the British, or rather the English, are very friendly, very polite, and there is a certain amount of reserve, which is pretty similar to the Swiss. I think what you said earlier in our conversation about island thinking is reflected in both cultures. However, due to the influence of Britain's former empire, and the melting pot that is London, the British have been exposed to diverse influences that they have made their own, whereas the Swiss are far less able to do that.

To return to Weingart at the Basel School of Design: as a teacher, he had a very strict methodology. The first exercise he made us do was to kern the word 'Basel' in Univers, 48 point, regular, all caps. It's a difficult word to kern because of the various character shapes. We had to work on it until we got it right, which meant that we would spend two or three days just kerning. Then, all of a sudden, you could just sense when it was right; you learned how to see. At Basel we did graphical translations of objects and my assignment was a wine glass, just a simple wine glass. The point was not to be able to draw the wine glass perfectly, the idea was to capture the essence of the wine glass, which could potentially be created with just one single line. I did 250 sketches of that wine glass. Again, and again, and again – until I began to look at it from different perspectives, to stop thinking of it as a wine glass and focus on its essence. Once you reach that point you no longer need to practice. If I had to create a wine glass now I wouldn't be able to draw it properly – my object drawing skills are not very good – but, within an hour, I could capture the essence of what a wine glass is, and, if given another hour, I could also get it right.

DC: That's significant in the context of our discussion on nationalism and design: this idea that somehow one is shaping an identity. In your practice, were you able to attain a sense of a global language, to step back from this Swiss typography thing?

BM: One thing should be noted regarding the concept of Swiss culture, or Swiss thinking within a graphic design context: I would say that it is definitely a German Swiss context. If you ask a French-speaking Swiss, they will have a completely different conception of what 'Swiss' is;

talk to someone from Ticino and they will also have their own take on the subject. This was particularly relevant when we did work for the Swiss television network SFR around 2012. The project was led by a German Swiss team. I collaborated closely with Alex Hefter, the team lead and brand manager, and we had to ensure that the typeface design was contemporary and reflected the values of the French-speaking population in particular, especially since culturally they often felt over-shadowed by the German-speaking population. The Italian-speaking population of Ticino was a bit more relaxed about the whole thing. The project was culturally and politically sensitive and we needed to create an international design language that could successfully be applied across cultural divides. It needed a contemporary design with the engineering qualities that you associate with German Swiss design but that would also have that French flair.

DC: We're facing a pretty difficult moment now, for instance with Brexit. Switzerland is experiencing this huge Swiss design revival: everybody is starting to go back to black-and-white typography, Swiss grids, and Weingart. What do you think about that? Is it possible that British designers are also starting to go back to their roots?

BM: I don't think so since I think British design – specifically in multicultural cities such as London and Manchester – have always been the most important creative hubs in the world. I do believe that there is a creative quality that you find in London – in terms of design, fashion, music, architecture – that beats everything else around the world. Everything. The reason for this is that production standards in London are so high that the only way you can differen-tiate yourself is through better ideas, concepts and creativity. Anyone can execute the same essential print quality, the same animation quality. As a result, since people are so good at production, you need the leverage of creativity. This is why I think London is not going back towards what the Swiss did fifty years ago. In contrast, I think that because of the quite insular view of the world that prevails in Switzerland – I would almost call it a lazy approach as opposed to a worldview – it leads to an attitude: 'Oh Brockmann, Swiss typography, it's all safe. Our borders are safe, let's not change, it's safe. This is how we've done it for the last 150 years, it works.' Yes, it does work but it is not progress, it is not moving forward. Orson Welles put it nicely: the French had a revolution and decapitated their monarch, the Italians had a revolution, and the English invented the telephone... what did the Swiss ever invent? The cuckoo clock! I think that sums it up. As for the Swiss national anthem, *Trittst im Morgenrot Daher...* Fuck. Me! It is soul destroying. You listen to the Italian anthem *Italia, Italia,* or the French *Marseillaise*, and it makes you realise that all these nations who have peppy, engaging and stirring anthems are all nations that had revolutions – major revolutions, civil wars and everything. Those anthems were inspired by a turning point in the history of these cultures, a moment that defined the future. These moments would continue to be reflected in their design, fashion, food, music, everything. The Swiss never had a revolution. In the early 1800s, Napoleon came, occupied the place, then told the Swiss 'sorry guys, you have a loose federation of independent states; that's no good; this is not how to run a state. *This* is how to run a state.' Essentially, Napoleon gave us what we are today. Napoleon basically said 'this is how we organise a government'. The Swiss simply adopted that, without a revolution. Nothing has changed since. Ever. Despite the fact that we have direct democracy and we go out to vote four times a year, nothing changes. Well, it changes, but ever so slowly.

DC: Yes, that is the safe way, always growing but slowly.

BM: Exactly, this is why the Swiss still do this Swiss typography stuff. They cannot move beyond that. Whereas I think British design will continue to evolve and adapt to new influences, be they technological, cultural, etc. What I mean is, yes we do have Brexit, which is a very unfortunate thing, but I don't think it will affect culture. Brexit or no, London if not the rest of Britain, will always be a hub. Obviously, much will depend on the outcome and how easy it will be for talent to get to London, but people are resourceful. I remember when I first arrived, since Switzerland is not in the EU, and bilateral agreements didn't exist, I had to have work permits. I had to get visas and all that. If you want it, you can make it happen. It is painful and tedious but you can make it happen. British design will continue to evolve, take for instance the work we have done with the BBC. The BBC's design language was truly cemented in the early 1990s when Martin Lambie-Nairn introduced the three squares and Gill Sans as the corporate typeface. This was a landmark event in corporate design. It retained emotional and traditional values while creating a contemporary look and feel. The logo was updated once to replace the italic style BBC to roman style lettering.

Gill Sans itself epitomises British design: it is quintessentially British. It is very difficult to put that into words. You can also observe that Britishness in the design for the London Underground by Edward Johnston who was Gill's teacher, so you can see what influenced Gill Sans. Both designs have a strong calligraphic quality and are quite sculptural, very Arts & Crafts which I mean in a very positive way. This visual identity succeeded in establishing the BBC as the very icon of a British institution. The challenge for us and the team at BBC GEL (Global Experience Language) was to take that Britishness into the 21st century, to make it pertinent in the 21st century. We needed to capture the expression of what is inherently British, make it super functional and, at the same time, fit for use on mobile devices, and other future technologies.

We conducted workshops with the teams at the BBC using exercises with imagery to define what Britishness is. The results were interesting: for instance, Burberry is British as a fashion style, Savile Row is British. If you see a Savile Row suit compared to an Italian suit from Milan, you can see the differences, feel the differences. Both of them are exquisite, but there's a different expression to them, the lines are different, the cut is slightly different. It's that kind of thing, that detail. We tried to visually define the essence of what makes something quintessentially British. If you compare the typeface that we designed for the BBC – BBC Reith – with Gill Sans, you can see there are connection points. It's the great grandchild of Gill Sans. Gill Sans wasn't used as a starting point but BBC Reith has the same genealogy and it is now a typeface that is fit for purpose. It captures the essence of the Arts and Crafts movement, very classic proportions and classic detailing. Certain design details may look familiar but you cannot quite make out what it is; like when you meet someone and you sense that you have seen them before.

When BBC Reith was introduced we hardly received any comments. This means that people didn't notice the change of typographic expression and simply viewed BBC Reith as if it had been there for a long time, that it was part of the BBC fabric. I take this as a great compliment. It proves that I did my job as a designer. People didn't see the typeface but simply read it. This reinforces the point that we are designers, not artists, and that Swiss typography is not about the result but the methodology, the rigour of solving a problem. It also shows that the British have the ability, despite established traditions and somewhat insular thinking, to step past their shadow and project themselves into the future, and to be influenced and be open to change.

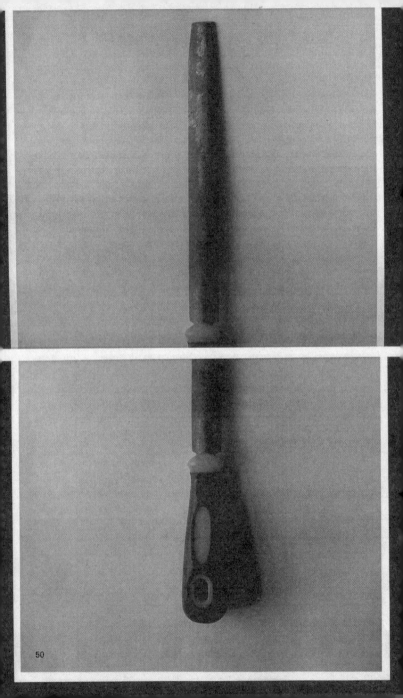

a

a

Fraser Muggeridge

DEMIAN CONRAD: We have always shared a common passion for the art of printmaking. Last time we met we were printing some big letter on screen printing at the Barbican. What have you brought here to show me?

FRASER MUGGERIDGE: I've brought the book, *Das Grosse Drei-Farben-Mischbuch in 50 Buch und 50 Offsetdrucken* by Hans Gaensslen. It was printed in 1959, and, as far as I know, it is a printer's specimen (page 68–70) from a Swiss printer. It has got some examples of how to combine colours. There's one in particular that I really like, and it's a key object for me because it shows how, with three plates, you can make sixteen variations which you can then turn around four times with sixty-four different images. In my opinion, this had a lot of impact: here I'm referring to the influence of Swiss graphic design in terms of printing and print production, not simply Swiss graphic design, as in visuals. I would like to know more about that whole world. You know more about all that than I do. It seems that [the Swiss] have a reputation, not only for excellence but also for experimentation? There is also a tradition of printing manuals, or specimens. You know, people are still doing them now, maximising their colour, Pantone® colours. It still happens today. I don't know if this printer still exists, or even if it is a printer. Actually, the design is not really that impressive now but it would have been quite impressive at the time. It's also nice that it's in three languages – English, German and French. This isn't the only one of these books, there are a few. It's like the chicken and the egg... what comes first? Is it the printer making them, then the designers appropriating the ideas? Or it is the designers who are making them and getting them out to the printer to disseminate them, I don't know. Probably a bit of both, right?

DC: One thing that's come up over the course of these conversations is that it seems more easy to negotiate and mull over ideas with Swiss printers than those in the UK, do you think that has changed?

FM: It depends where they are, and where you are. I guess there's a tradition now in the UK regarding the books we make – we would never print a book in London. We rarely print books in the UK. We always print in a different country, because of quality and cost I guess. If you were printing a book, you might just possibly print it in the town in which you're designing it, right? We would have to go all the way to Stoney Hill or somewhere like that. Which we could do, but then you can't muck around too much, say try a different colour for the layers, or whatever. Yeah, this is a good book. This is the key. I've definitely used it in my work, this idea of twisting, and then the idea that, if you have three combinations to start with, you can use them to create all these new variations.

DC: I remember Italian graphic designer Leonardo Sonnoli did a few projects that way. It seems to be a little bit like Muriel Cooper's rotary offset prints or Max Bill's variation posters?

FM: Such techniques might have existed in England but they have never been documented. I imagine there's this notion of craft and artisans with printers in Switzerland? A feeling of quality, craft, design, which I guess is very unique to your country. I would imagine, I don't know! How do you think things have progressed since then? There's this sort of traditional Swiss, or modern-day Swiss design, with lots of Helvetica. This book was probably pre-Pantone®. I don't know enough about printing history to know when Pantone® colours were introduced. I think it was like a 1960s, 1970s sort of American thing – but I expect every country would have had their own colour system. What about your project with water? Water printing? How did that come about? What made you think about squirting water into a machine? It must have come from somewhere that had more to do with printing, or knowing that you can use water or water and ink, or the little things the printers have, those little squirty things?

DC: Yes, I call it Water Random Offset Printing. I was influenced by the process used by John Cage. He has always been a great inspiration for me. It's pretty simple: before becoming a graphic designer, I was trained as a *Schriftsetzer*, a typesetter. I worked closely with a printer, and spent four years of my apprenticeship at an offset printing press. I learned all about the plates, washing up, developer, liquids, all sorts of stuff.

FM: It's more about the idea that you can have the same design but execute it in a variety of styles – this book uses the same style. One [of the illustrations] is a solid colour, one is a dot raster version, another looks like a kind of hand marker, and one appears more like it's painted. You could say they are all the effects of the same design and I like the idea that it's all about graphic representation. It's a style: you can do spot colour, greyscale, dot colour, you can do a picture of it, or you can do a painting of it. It's a bit like that project that I showed you, where people were making copies of my posters. I think there is something to potentially develop in this respect.

DC: Did you ever receive interns or colleagues from Switzerland at your studio here in London?

FM: No, never. It's something I've always thought about, but no one from Switzerland had ever really approached me. You know, Switzerland might be one of the only places in Europe where I've never given a talk, or a workshop. Perhaps they look at my work and they just don't like it, or don't know it. Be that as it may, no one from Switzerland has ever come to the studio. Maybe it's just a matter of exposure, maybe students don't see my work..?

DC: So let's look at it from another angle: back in the past, when you were at university, were there any Swiss around?

FM: No. As you know, I went to Reading University in the 1990s, I don't think there were any Swiss people around, but we definitely studied the work of [Josef] Müller-Brockmann, Jan Tschichold, Karl Gerstner and [Max] Bill. They taught us about the debate between Bill and Tschichold, the big row and this kind of fallout that they had and whether it was real or not and all that sort of stuff. But no, there was no one who was actually Swiss. We were introduced to people like Wolfgang Weingart as part of design history, but we were not taught about what was going on in contemporary Swiss design, it was all some-what pre-Internet. You didn't see much Swiss graphic design around in the early 1990s. We did go on a trip to Basel. We travelled through

Basel on the way to Italy on a university trip, to Rome and Florence, to look at lettering. As a young person, I remember it was amazing. There was lots of graffiti there, which surprised me – loads of it along the train tracks, loads of this really cool graffiti and it had this edge of preciseness.

FM: How would you describe British graphic design at the time you were a student? Who were the icons of British graphic design for you at that time?

DC: There were definitely a few who were quite influential. When I was a student, the most influential was perhaps Neville Brody. I remember spending hours trying to replicate the blurry typeface composition he was doing. It was quite a relief for us because we are so into precision and structure – we feel a lot of pressure from our Calvinist culture. The general idea is to be correct and, if you work hard during your life you earn your way to paradise.

FM: So how did Weingart play into that? When you look at Weingart's stuff from the 1960s, he's still got precision, he's also got this playfulness. To my mind, he is the pioneer of new wave typography. Do you agree?

DC: That is probably the case. April Greiman took Armin Hoffman's classes in Basel, and Weingart was there. Even then, he was already starting to do his own thing and breaking the rules. What kind of influence did he have in London?

FM: I think that book… the big orange book, I can't remember what it's called – I think it's just called *Typography* – is pretty influential. I just remember those posters done in 1978 with the dots that kind of blend in, and the colour and the overlay. Cool, right? For us it was all about that book, *New Wave Typography* by Rick Poynor. The one everyone bought: it sold like 300,000 copies. That was a big book for us, really important. There wasn't much Swiss stuff in there actually, but it was a big book for me. New Wave graphic design, that was kind of where it was at.

DC: Do you think that Weingart might also have influenced Brody's approach to typography?

FM: Yes, I definitely think so… again, this is just my opinion, it's not backed up by any hard evidence, but I think Brody's work emerged from a mixture of punk, early New Wave and technology. However, it does not look like Weingart's. I recently bought a Fuse book: you know the Fuse Project? I remember it at the time, maybe ten years ago. Everyone thought the graphics were pretty lame, right? But I was reading it the other day and it has some really amazing ideas. Perhaps its looks and application of ideas are a bit 1990s, however the ideas I think are, unconsciously, similar to ideas I've had for these fonts that I make, where I hack things, or turn stuff around. There's a lot of that going on. I didn't really realise you can be influenced by things without even properly examining them, it might just be in the air. I think there's a lot of that going on. Like all this stuff on this wall here at the Ambit Gallery.

DC: You know, another interesting thing is that the British were in love with the Swiss Alps. Most Swiss tourists are British. St. Moritz is pretty British, and if you go to Verbier it's even more obvious. For instance Richard Branson, the owner of Virgin, has a huge mansion in Verbier and if you look back at the stories of the first Alpine sportsmen, they are mostly British.

FM: Oddly enough, my grandmother was brought up in Switzerland. Her parents, or her uncle – I can't be entirely sure – had been some of the first people to set up skiing holidays out of London. From England to Switzerland in the early 20th century – they were called Lunn Poly. I think it still exists today, perhaps as a sort of travel agency. The first ever British ski championship was held in Switzerland in 1926 – I'm not joking, it's true! – and my great great uncle, Leonard Dobbs, he won it. We have a picture of him skiing in Switzerland with his suit on and a pipe! So you're right, there is a connection to my family, my grandmother went to a Swiss finishing school. It was a school for girls called a finishing school. Not like print finishing, where you learn how to bind – that would have been good though! In the UK, often wealthy families would send their daughters to a Swiss finishing school where they would be taught how to walk, how to behave, how to socially engage with people. Anyway, it's got nothing to do with graphic design, but maybe it's got something to do with the precision. It's all linked. It's all about attitude. There's something about attitude that's quite important and yet, we are quite a gentle country – on the surface! We did have the British Empire, we tried to take over the world, right? However, you seem to be quite a polite country. Switzerland never did that. I don't think Switzerland has ever even had a colony?

DC: Never. The only military thing we are known for is the private military that protects the Pope in Rome: the Swiss Guard, a corps of mercenaries. We have always stuck quite solidly to our neutral position.

FM: So what's the situation today? When you think of Swiss graphic design, what do you think of?

DC: There's something quite funny – a few years ago, there was also a renaissance of traditional Swiss design, like in Britain. I'm thinking about Anthony Burrill's printing for instance, Arts and Crafts isn't it? He does not print himself, but delegates his work to a printer to do the typesetting, he has the idea and then... In Switzerland as well, we have young designers typesetting the way they used to in Weingart's time.

FM: Who is the guy who just did that book edited by Lars Müller? It's called *Type* [Editor's Note: actually *True Print*], and has an acetate cover. It's nice stuff. The author [Dafi Kühne] has a big letterpress studio. All that in the UK, I think, comes from people like Alan Kitching, you know Alan Kitching's work? He's been working since the 1980s, doing letterpress like that. Perhaps his message wasn't as strong as that of Anthony Burrill's, but he really revitalized that whole world and I think the renaissance in the UK with stuff like craft beer, brown bread, nice coffee, food markets, handmade clothes... I don't know, this idea of this duality of things. So we have our life of duality, we buy all our stuff from the supermarket, then, on a Saturday morning we go to the farmer's market to get our bread and it makes us feel good. In a way it's kind of similar for letterpress printing. We do all our stuff on InDesign all week and then we either go and buy a letterpress or we do a letterpress workshop. Perhaps this is also the reason for the rise of the Risograph, but you can't really experiment with it, since it's a really sophisticated Japanese machine and it has so many sensors. Have you ever used one? You can't really muck around with the inks. You can do a few things – I did something with my girlfriend Eleanor [Vonne Brown], we have a Riso at home, we put our Christmas tree over the Riso, on Christmas day. Riso, I think has changed the concept of small publishers, small printing, bright colours...

DC: It is interesting how some designers extend their practice over several disciplines. In the 1980s, Bruce Mau stated in an interview: "I'm going to drop the 'graphic' part of my title and just be a designer."

He wanted to be perceived as someone who could do more than just graphic design. So now there are a lot of graphic designers who do self-publishing, fashion, curating, interviewing, journalism, and the list goes on.

FM: I was amazed… have you seen this book, this green coloured book? It's a new book called *The History of Graphic Design in Switzerland*. It's really good; I was amazed when I looked through it – when I bought it, I thought it was going to be interesting. Then I opened up the spread and there were my projects, my curating project at the Delaware, this alternative form of graphic design, like a double-page spread. Really, it's a great book. It's not just about the history of graphic design, it's about the history of the exhibition of graphic design, and the display of graphic design, and not just in Switzerland. So I would definitely recommend it. It's got a green cover and a funny name, like *Another Book on the History of Swiss Graphic Design*, or something. You should really check it out. Let's talk about Gerstner, Bill, Müller-Brockmann, Emil Ruder – I'm sure there's another one I've forgotten about – do you think these people were actually pioneers, or do you think that they were considered pioneers because of books they wrote that gave them exposure, and went on to become the canon? Do you know what I mean? Are they only considered pioneers because other graphic designers have written about them, and they have now been regurgitated in a big long circle?

DC: Yes. I think that they gave us some basic tools that enabled us to industrialise the process of graphic design. Also methodology: before things were more messy and instinctive. They provided structure, something that was easy to absorb and understand, a standard.

FM: They bestowed all that through writing, teaching and working. When I think of our contribution to the history of graphic design, I feel the need to leave some kind of legacy: in a sense, that always takes the form of some kind of printed book, right?

DC: Yes, or perhaps in the future there will be videos on YouTube?

FM: Sure. In fact, I do have an idea that I think is really good and I'm amazed it hasn't been done before… maybe you can be part of it? It's basically a TV series, six programmes about the history of graphic design. Has that ever been done?

DC: There is this guy – he's an illustrator...what's his name? [Editor's Note: James Victore] He's a New Yorker, and he has a YouTube channel and talks about how to become a designer. There are some people who are trying to make graphic design videos. However, in Switzerland for instance, if you are a successful graphic designer, you tend not to have an online profile. There is this attitude, you know? Mainly it's again connected to this Calvinist culture, but you need to come from a more open and extroverted culture in order to do something like this YouTube thing.

FM: Still, I think graphic design is entering the mainstream. People now have opinions, everyone has InDesign on their computer, everyone knows what a typeface is, anyone can design their own presentation, it's so engrained in society. So, I'm thinking TV programmes, a series of six histories of theory, location, etc.

DC: You run a typography summer school that is quite international, and which has exposed you to the educational perspectives of many countries. What do you think is missing today in the schools?

FM: That's a good question. In my opinion, there are a few things. There is what is missing – this is a really big generalisation, mind you – in the UK I think there's a major focus on idea generation, thinking, critical thinking, coming up with ideas, and I think that's great, I don't have a problem with that. However, what is often lacking in these schools is a basic approach to hierarchy, alignment, leading, teaching how to choose a typeface or how to make something of craft. Not craft as in cutting something out with scissors, but crafting on the Mac. How to do something properly using the software that we're currently using. I do think that's a bit lacking in British design schools. I think perhaps that people, rightly so in many ways, are expected to pick this up themselves and muddle through. It's a bit like learning how to drive a car: if you had to learn it completely by yourself it would be really difficult. You need to be told things like 'you need to put it in second gear now'. My feeling is that everyone can have really good ideas, but part of graphic design is about visualising that idea. Knowing how to work with type and not be scared of it, or not to think that manually setting text is boring or beneath you. You want the big idea. I think there's a lot of emphasis on this cultural commentator. We're all very clever, we can all talk about culture and meta design, but actually it comes down to us making something that's well crafted and that can look good. In a sense, that's what I perceived would be the focal point of the summer school, as well as how to make briefs that are relevant. We always did live projects where they had a real job, a real task. It is important to learn to deal with the challenge of a real task. We do initiate projects, but you don't do that as your job, that's only part of your job. Your main job is working for a client who says 'we need this' and then you make it happen, and come back with 'Here's some content, or here's a space, or here's the brief': your job is to package the content. Again, I think this type of project should be more encouraged within schools, so students can learn about printing, about how to talk about their work, how to deal with it when someone says 'oh, I don't like that', or 'it's not right' and I also think that the printing process needs to be used a bit more. There are some great facilities in these schools and they need to make better use of them. Like some of the jobs you've done and some of the jobs I've done, students should be practising the printing process, using it as an idea, as a way to create work, rather than just moving shapes around on a screen. That's what I think about British education at the moment.

DC: I also wanted to ask you about the design and market culture. Your design projects are freer, compared to the rigid structure of the Swiss. How do you think your style might work in the Swiss market?

FM: Perhaps that is why I've never been approached by them! I think there are instances of Swiss graphic designers doing stuff that is more free. Like Maximage – they are definitively pushing the envelope, and some of your random stuff is definitely mixing both ends of the spectrum, right? They have typography that's left justified and pure and stripped back and minimal, but within that they also have got a kind of image-making thing going on. To get back to my work, I really don't know. To be honest, I don't think it would fit in there. Perhaps that's the reason why no one from Switzerland ever applied to my studio.

DC: That's interesting. Why do you think it fits in here so well, then? It also seems that what you are doing is working really well for you here more recently: you are working on a lot of interesting and important projects. Why do you think what you do here in London works?

FM: That's a good question. I think my work is maybe an antidote for work, that is... I've got another theory, namely that it's quite easy now to be a graphic designer. It's quite easy to make something look OK because InDesign is quite easy to use now, much easier than it used to be. It's all automated stuff, and I think you see a lot of good graphic design in the UK, it's just really good. There are a lot of great students coming out and it's all good. Still, for me, I used to do that kind of stuff, like the Reading stuff, or make things just look good, and then I thought, surely now I need to get to another level. I'm at a certain level and I need to do something either higher or lower than the norm. I think that's when I started to mess things up a bit through work with artists. I've been working with, say Fiona Banner or Jeremy Deller, in this kind of relationship between art and design, where I'm not a graphic designer to whom an artist gives their material to make a book, we're collaborating together on it. I think that's had a big influence on me. I used to work with designers, they used to send me an InDesign file and it was all over the place, and I used to always tidy it up. Now I just carry on and it stays all over the place and I think that's been a big shift. I think it works for me within the very small niche that I'm in. However, it does not work for me in the mainstream, it doesn't even work for me with bigger jobs, because I might do this stuff that's a bit off, or as we might say, 'knowingly wrong'. Clients would then say 'it looks horrible', or 'I don't like it'. That happens a lot. I would even get comments like 'are you on drugs?', 'are you ok?' or 'go home'. So, in a way I'm just existing, probably like you or most graphic designers, in a really small bubble, somewhere just left of reality. I'm not working for a coffee shop or a bank. I think I'm playing on the vernacular, or the weirdness of British quirkiness. I'm trying to bring that to graphic design to make things look a bit off. I can only do that because I know I can mix that with something very rigorous – it's not just off and all over the place, it's off but it might be beautifully typeset, or be an interesting production. It's about that kind of knowledge, that double edge – always schizophrenic, that's what I'm trying to do at the moment.

DC: Having spent one week in Brick Lane, I think I got that and I understand why you approach things in that way. A whole other feeling pervades the place – the city with its integration of many diverse cultures. From those influences emerges this vernacular and beautiful typesetting, like a Vietnamese sign on the corner here where the designer had to squeeze in the type because there was no space left! You sense a culture made here by the people that is quite unique.

FM: Absolutely. We do tend to forget that. I went to the Lebanese shops in Edgware Road to ask them where they get their kebab shop paper from, because I'm really into that. I'm definitely influenced by multiculturalism. This shirt is made by a Bangladeshi tailor in East London. I think that's perhaps a big difference as opposed to Switzerland, since Switzerland doesn't really have any immigration policy. That's a whole debate right there. Still, if you look outside of London, you will probably see something a little bit different. However, this is Brick Lane: in the 1920s it was very Jewish, I don't know if you've seen the synagogue? Then in the 1950s and 1960s, it became more Pakistani, Indian, and, up the road, you've got Turkish… you've got this mix of cultures, which to me is what makes London great.

DC: For sure, that's something I love about London. As a Swiss, it's a breath of fresh air…like, wow. It shakes you up a little bit. In light of the recent political and economic situation, and the problems that the UK has been facing, what's your take on Brexit and how do you think Brexit is going to affect the creative industry here?

FM: Potentially, who knows? We don't. Obviously, most studios employ people from abroad; even in our studio at the moment, we have someone from France, someone interning from Belgium, and a young designer from Colombia. Upstairs, there are people from Korea, Germany, Austria… Within our studio, there's a wide range of people from different places, which is great. Obviously if Brexit means they all can't work here for whatever reason, which seems to be what people are talking about, then it's a big problem. For us, it also means issues in terms of our trade and it might be a problem when say, I'm working with a printer in Estonia – we work with a lot of printers in Estonia – just to get stuff delivered, just to get though another form of customs, the practical problems are going to be a pain in the arse. For instance, at the moment, we had to deliver something to, say Norway. I don't think Norway is in the European Union? I'm pretty sure it was Norway and I didn't know that and we sent some books there and they were just taxed in and out. For me, Brexit is about closing doors when the world should actually be opening doors. We should be making it easier to come and live here and for me to go and live elsewhere, for me to print in Estonia and for you to design a project in Japan or whatever. It should be easier and Brexit seems to be going backwards. So I think it's not good. I suppose it's ultimately a problem with people outside of London not wanting to embrace all this, that's what it is. It's not even about immigration really. I think it's like a fake news thing that somehow actually came to happen.

THE GRA

E

HANS GAENSSLEN

LE GRAN

Freda Sack

DEMIAN CONRAD: It seems you have many interesting little objects with you, perhaps we can start with you telling me about one of those?

FREDA SACK: These items are my personal ones: in the mid-1990s we invited Josef Müller-Brockmann over to London to give a lecture at the International Society of Typographic Designers (ISTD), as part of a lecture series. We had lots of really interesting people come over and we held some of the lectures at the St Bride Printing Library. Later, when there was more demand, we used the Royal Institute of British Architects (RIBA). There was a huge demand for Müller-Brockmann. It was quite a mixed group since, as you know, Swiss design had a major impact on British design in the 1960s. Many designers from that generation were very much influenced by the Swiss International Style. They perceived it as a breath of fresh air during what I think Professor Ian McLaren qualified as the dark days of British design, referring to the postwar period. Even a decade after the end of the war, British design was still very traditional, fairly craft-based. You had this whole era of designers such as McLaren, and also Colin Forbes of Pentagram, who were very much influenced by Swiss style. Also, a lot of educators were really interested in the process. I think that was quite significant at the time since they were young, professional designers who then went on to become teachers of design. There were a handful of them who were very much taken with the Swiss International Style. They went on to study the process behind it and use it as a basis for their teaching, particularly at colleges like Ravensbourne. There were certain teachers there like Geoffrey White. If you ever get the chance to go and visit Geoff White, he's just an amazing man. He's 89 and he still goes to the London College of Communication on a regular basis to give little talks to the students about his work. He was incredibly influenced by Swiss design and it is the basis of his teaching. This in turn marked a whole generation, and even a second generation, of designers in fact, since he taught from the late 1960s, or early 1970s onwards. Consequently, many really good designers were taught by him and that is the basis of their graphic design. The really good tutors then mentor the next generation of designers and so it goes. On the ISTD blog there is a piece about Geoff White, and at the end of the blog there are a lot of comments from students from different generations about his teaching style, which was based on the Swiss style.

So, again, back in the mid-1980s, we invited Müller-Brockmann over and it was a mixed audience of people that already knew him and these younger designers who were being taught by people who knew his work. It was something of a cult following at the time, so much so that we generally held the talks at the Royal Institute of British Architects; we just had the big lecture theatre and we usually only had the front part open but it could open up to hold 400 people and we actually had to do that for this talk. This was the invitation (page 84) – I feel so lucky to have been able to meet and talk to him. He was really quite a humble man. We produced the newsletter number 77 about the lecture and the visit (page 82). There are lots of really nice quotes in there. It talks about why we were doing the lectures: it was at the time when my partner David Quay and myself were the co-chairs of ISTD; overseeing it and coordinating the lecture series was part of the work we were doing at the time. To this day, I still don't know how we managed to do it all without the technology that we have now – it was pre-Mac, pre-mobile phone. We've also had Wim Crouwel in to speak several times. The issue number 78, which is the issue that came out right after that one, contains a letter from Müller-Brockman's wife Shizuko Yoshikawa (page 85). She was an artist in her own right. In fact, she came over a few years later as a judge for our professional design awards. She gave me a book of her work which is absolutely beautiful: beautiful colours, and paintings.

DC: You had known Müller-Brockmann previously, right?

FS: Well, I had known his work and was aware of his influence because I'm a typographer by training. I was at university in the late 1960s to early 1970s and we had some very good lecturers within the print community. They were passing on some of the inspirational work that they had come across, mostly by Müller-Brockmann. It was his posters: they were so minimal, stripped down. In most cases, they almost entirely consisted of typography with no images... this whole thing about the minimalism of design, just using one typeface. Generally, one side is in black and white. This was the whole basis of the teaching at the time. They became exercises in which, if you could deal with typography in that manner, then you could blow away those boundaries if you wanted to and do other things. Still, you had to learn how to make use of restrictions.

His work was featured in articles in magazines like *Grey Magazine* and *Graphics International*. As you know, magazines and books were the only way we got information at the time. This has become grubby: this is a book (page 83) Müller-Brockmann gave me as a present when he left; he signed it as well, which is lovely. We obviously had books by AGI members, and Müller-Brockmann was a member. As a result, there were quite a few really good books on poster design to which we had access.

DC: That's funny because you have said that today design is so crowded and saturated. It's difficult to imagine that period...

FS: I think it really appealed to people interested in typography. There are several ways of looking at typography: one is seeing it as purely about the detail and the technology. I see it as encompassing far more than that. In my view, typography is the main building block of graphic design. It's essentially how graphic design is structured. It's about the grid, the materials, the use of space and the way that you communicate. I don't think you can be a good graphic designer if you are not a good typographer.

DC: That's a great statement. During the 1970s, when you were finishing up with your studies, were there other Swiss designers who were also coming to London?

FS: Yes, I met a few. When I left college I went to work for Letraset, one of the foremost type design companies at the time. I know it sounds bizarre now since it's quite a basic system of creating letters, but we used to bring out ranges of new typefaces and we had a panel of rather famous designers who helped pick the ones that we were going to put into the Letragraphica series. This was our flagship collection; typefaces

Freda Sack

were released maybe four times a year, and they were picked by a panel, made up of people like Derek Birdsall... I'm trying to think of the other people that were on it. We had international designers on the panel. I remember Massimo Vignelli for one, perhaps because he's American... I'm sure there was another Italian – could have been Italian or another Swiss – I can't remember, it was a long time ago.

DC: I always try to understand how cultures disseminate, it's a big interest of mine. As we discuss the advent of this new Swiss methodology, and the simplification that characterised it, would you say it became a sort of mania?

FS: Indeed. I know that people like Emil Ruder were hugely influential as well.

DC: How interesting. I have just received a letter (page 125) to Richard Hollis from Emil Ruder which says he was invited to come here but couldn't make it. During your studies as a typographer, can you explain the effect that Helvetica had when it was first released here? What were the initial reactions to it?

FS: When I was at college, we were already using Grotesque quite a lot, as well as Helvetica, so they were already established typefaces for me. I did meet Max Miedinger once, the person that created Helvetica, and that was a privilege. I've been very lucky to have met lots of interesting people over the course of my career. The typography community is quite a small world and is made up of genuinely nice people. In many ways, it was easier back then for people to meet face to face with some of these major figures. There was a period, I guess around the 1980s, when some graphic designers became superstars and then things became really different, more like a pop culture. It was interesting because Lars Müller came over as well, and the lecture took the form of Lars Müller interviewing Müller-Brockmann. The lecture consisted of Lars introducing Josef, and talking with him. There was one point, and I can't remember exactly whether it was a question that came up or a point in the lecture itself, but suddenly David Carson came up, and I think Müller-Brockmann turned around and introduced him to the crowd, and the whole audience erupted because at the time he was a cult figure. Carson was the absolute antithesis of Müller-Brockmann: he wasn't really a graphic designer or a typographer at all, just someone who happened to be doing a magazine that was very trendy and he was just cutting out bits and pieces and throwing it against a page. There are even quotes from various people who said that, despite the fact that Müller-Brockmann's work did not appeal to them on an aesthetic level, they did appreciate his process.

DC: Around the same time, British style often made use of fonts such as Gill Sans, what did you think about that?

FS: Gill Sans seems to have stood the test of time. I think particularly in London, it's almost like the iconic typeface of London, because it's so engrained within the transport system and all that side of things. Also, it continues to be used a lot in books. In fact, Derek Birdsall used Gill a lot and he also used Joanna, another typeface by Eric Gill, along with it.

DC: I read somewhere that it's sort of the Helvetica of Britain.

FS: I suppose you could say that, yes.

DC: Perhaps with a more humanistic touch?

DC: I like the fact that, when you started out, in your twenties, you used to draw one line after another by hand until the curve was just perfect. Do you still practice your craft in this manner?

FS: That's how I started out, I used to draw the letters by hand on paper and then cut them out. Back then, you had to draw every single letter of the alphabet, including the punctuation.

DC: So you must be sensitive to every kind of line and curve that you see around your environment?

FS: Yes. There is a unique connection when you do or draw something by hand. That hand-to-eye connection is quite unique. My eyesight is not so brilliant now, but once upon a time, it was possible for me to actually trim a sliver off a curve as thin as a human hair to improve it, and to perceive just how it improved the curve.

DC: Amazing, you have passed through many changes in technology. Can you tell me about it?

FS: First I worked with hot metal and then I worked at Letraset, where we used rubbed-out instant lettering transfers and then I went into photo-typesetting. That was like a two-inch box, so they were very quick to make. Basically, you would do eighty characters – capitals, lower case, numbers and punctuation. We would make them very quickly, we would draw them quite small and then make little cuts of them; then they would make a negative to create a two-inch film font. So it was reel-to-reel: I don't know if you've ever seen any of those. That was headline photosetting, and it was all the rage in the late 1970s to early 1980s, especially in advertising. I would sometimes be commissioned to draw and create a typeface for advertising and I would have a week to do it. I would do a special font and then that required high-end machines for linotype stencils. They would be quite big: each letter would be reversed out of the centre of the rubric we would cut and that would act as a photo negative which would fit on camera, linotype or stencil and be transferred at the other end, onto something that small on a typesetting machine. That would be a frisket. Often they would be cut in reverse as well. You would cut out a rubric of a letter and that would have to be in reverse as well. We often had to cut little nicks out of the corners, and they were terrible to cut: you could only do it standing up because they would get caught on you.

DC: What's your take on new technologies such as parametric typefaces, or new versions of metafonts?

FS: I know. It's just so easy to create a typeface now, and most people don't create from scratch. They will take something and amend it: there is very little real, original typeface design there. It starts to look quite bland and everything begins to have a similar look to it because the proportions don't change. People tend not to change the proportions so a lot of typefaces look very similar. People get fixated on certain ideas and then you just have variations of those same ideas. It's actually really difficult to design an original sans-serif, because you don't have much to play with. I did something for Swiss International Airlines, creating a typeface based on that lettering. You can look at it and say, well it looks like it's ready to go – it looks that way – it's really difficult because we did design it from scratch.

DC: What were your expectations when you started that project?

FS: In the beginning we were only going to design a type logo, which was 'International' or just the word 'Swiss' actually, which is the most difficult word for anybody to draw because it's got three 'S's in it and 'S' is one of the most difficult characters to balance. Also from our point of view, it was fine if you were just going to draw 'Swiss' like that but then it's got to wrap around an aeroplane fuselage on a curve, and you've got curve after curve – then you've got all the different curves. You've got the Jumbo curve, the 747 curve and you have to draw them for different sizes, but also consider that it will go on a sugar wrapper, timetables, registration screens, that sort of thing. So, you have to consider all the different technologies in which it has to work, and also when you're looking at the word on an aeroplane, you might be looking at the word – you might be in an airport lounge looking out at it as a banner or you might be on the ground looking up. So it's always going to look different, especially with all those 'S's. Very few letters are as difficult to balance. So, it started off with the word 'Swiss' and then when you had to extend it into other languages, into the Swiss language, the letter forms increase in number because you have to cover the languages. Then they ended up asking us for an entire typeface.

DC: How did you prototype this project? Did you make like a 3D mock-up to check in a real situation?

FS: The agency we were working with [Winkreative] created a painted mock-up aeroplane and, as is usual with these things, they always want that sort of thing in a hurry, so there was a press conference and they were releasing the image and it made headlines. We worked mainly with a chap named Erik Torstensson. He's been in the press quite recently: he was a bit of a character, married to some society lady. There was something in the *Sun* the other week. It was very funny, actually. They called him her 'boy-toy'. I never saw him as a boy-toy, but I did come into contact with the man later. It was quite funny because Bruno Maag and I started working about the same time on one of our very first typefaces – he did the technology for NatWest bank, the original NatWest bank font. Then, gradually, we began moving in different directions, and ended up becoming business rivals. We were always up against each other for the same jobs, or we would be quoting on the same jobs over and over again. It was quite interesting because I thought, 'I'm never going to get the Swiss job because Bruno is Swiss and I'm not.' However, to my surprise, we actually got the job, and it was a really interesting job on which to work.

DC: Yes, I remember, there were some people who didn't like it, who felt that it was less minimalist that it could have been.

FS: I have to admit that working with Winkreative was different, they were media people, not really pure typographers. For instance the cross was not designed on a grid so it was quite difficult to align the name.

DC: Yes, I had some similar experiences. My studio did a series for Art Basel that was a one-shot, an experimental Swiss campaign. Previously Hess & Muller had done their posters, and they did have something in common with Whitechapel Gallery: the typography, a sort of minimalistic identity.

FS: That Hess & Muller poster was something that could be reused, they printed something and overprinted it for a variety of things, and it ended up different each time. I think that's the story... There are some really beautiful pieces of work in this book, for instance with Studio Dumbar. Dutch design has also had a huge influence in the UK.

DC: Really? Do you think that it is more influential than Swiss design?

FS: No, I think Swiss design has undoubtedly had more of an impact. In a way, I hate to say this, since we really kind of introduced Dutch design into the UK when we were doing our lectures. We knew a lot about Dutch design because we had friends and colleagues in Holland. We saw a lot of what was going on and it has a slight quirkiness to it – it's more minimalist than English design but also more influenced by Bauhaus. Still, it also retains very distinctive Dutch characteristics. I know a lot of Dutch designers and we had quite a few of them come over to speak, and we also had people from the Dutch Post Office, who were big design clients. People like that are huge influences on design, and this is why I think the London Transport System were the biggest commissioners of design ever because they had people creating posters, from the 1920s, 1930s, 1940s onwards and they commissioned a famous artist to do them. The same goes for the Dutch Post Office, albeit in a different way in Holland: they were essentially commissioners of design.

DC: I see new generations of designers ushering in a big revival in Swiss style. What do you think about the concept of national design nowadays? It is still relevant?

FS: I think there is still an element of that. I think you see it sometimes in this country, where quite a lot of people, like Alan Kitching, for example, are going back to letterpress printing. He has a huge following. There are a number of young designers who are setting up their own letterpress workshops. There is also this thing about using your hands, making things, which is important. I think people have become a bit disenchanted with sitting in front of a screen for over six or seven hours a day. I've seen some universities where they don't allow their students to touch a computer for the first six months or so. In places where there is access to metal type and letterpress and practical things, there also seems to be more flexibility, more imagination used in terms of working with materials. I think that, with everything onscreen these days, people have lost touch with the tactile quality of things. Before the advent of digital, everything was photographed and printed, and I feel you can tell the difference. They also don't know how to work with printers. A lot of designers of a certain generation have probably never been to a printer or seen something on press, checked the colours, checked the ink. They don't know anything about it. There's also a thing about paper as well. The feel of different paper stocks. So many paper companies are going bust and so many of the really good printers have gone bust – there were several amazing printers in Holland that people used to use.

DC: Is there something else you want to add about this relationship between these two countries?

FS: I still believe that the influence of Swiss design is very strong and important. I think that hopefully we still have enough good tutors who will continue to teach in that way because it really does underpin design and the people that get it are the ones that fly. They are also the ones that really understand typography. If they are taught by good people, they will go on to perpetuate that tradition.

The newsletter of the International
Society of Typographic Designers

Summer 1996

77

TypoGraphic News

On Thursday 23rd May, the STD hosted a lecture given by Josef Müller-Brockmann. When this issue containing extracts and quotes from that remarkable occasion was just about to go to press, we heard the sad news of his death, and so we dedicate the issue to this truly special man.

'As a young person I had no clear perception of my future—I only knew that my professional career depended on my energy, self-criticism, discipline and a permanent desire to learn.' Josef Müller-Brockmann 1914–1996

JOSEF MÜLLER-BROCKMANN
ヨゼフ・ミューラー＝ブロックマン

To Freda Sack

with warm regard

Josef Müller - Brockmann

The std presents Josef Müller-Brockmann
talking about the influences on his work
as part of their 96 lecture series. Lars Müller
the editor and publisher of the book
Josef Müller-Brockmann Pioneer of Swiss
Graphic Design, will introduce the lecture.
A new paperback edition will be on sale
on the night with signed copies available.

Thursday 23rd May at 6.30 pm

RIBA
66 Portland Place
London W1N 4AD

std members £8.00
non-members £10.00
students £5.00

Josef Müller-Brockmann
Pioneer of Swiss Graphic Design

To reserve a seat contact
David Quay or Freda Sack

Studio 12
10–11 Archer Street
London W1V 7HG

T 0171 734 6925
F 0171 734 2607

Cheques made payable to
Society of Typographic Designers

The Müller-Brockmann lecture was a very popular event, some of the letters of appreciation are shown below.

Look out for lecture dates in 1997 because from November we go Dutch.

12

Panegyrics

Honorary Fellowship

The STD is very grateful that Lars Müller and Josef Müller-Brockmann made the trip to England at such short notice to give the lecture.

Müller-Brockmann has since been elected Honorary Fellow to the STD. This is awarded in recognition of outstanding typographic design of international significance.

The man himself

dear david and freda
thank you very much for your kind letter also i thank you very much for your electing me as an honorary fellow of the std. we wish you both and your staff a more sunny sommer!

sincerely yours
josef müller-brockmann,
shizuko yoshikawa

From all at studio 12

It was with great sadness that we received the news that Josef Müller-Brockmann died on the 30th August. We consider it a great privilege that he agreed to come to London to give a talk for the STD. Judging from the views on this page we are sure this is a reaction shared by many designers. We have known and admired his work for a long time, and we were honoured to meet and talk to the man in person.

We know from a recent conversation with his publisher, Lars Müller, that Müller-Brockmann was very happy that he had talked to and got a good response from the young designers in this country. This was what he wanted and achieved.

His publisher

Dear Freda, dear David... The Müller-Brockmann event was a great experience. Congratulations for the perfect planning and the success, which is also yours.

Kind regards Lars Müller

Thank you and a few suggestions

Thank you for organizing the Josef Müller-Brockmann lecture. It was inspiring to be in the presence of such an influential yet modest person.

I have some sympathy with the comments you expressed at the end of the evening regarding David Carson and P. Scott Makela but felt that Lars Müller's initial reluctance to pick up the gauntlet then sideways swipe, 'we can't all be as "talented" as David Carson but we can all be as talented as Müller-Brockmann', was more effective.

Müller-Brockmann gave fundamental thinking to graphic design—quality was apparent in his work and unlike many examples today did not need to be intellectualized. it was powerful, you knew it by looking at it.

I would like to be kept in touch with further STD events which I will publicize to the students at the LCP as part of the 're-addressing the balance' it would be wonderful to have lectures by- Ott and Stein, Odermatt and Tissi (recently profiled in Graphics International), Baumann and Baumann, Armin Hofmann, Jacqueline Cassey (MIT), Willi Kunz, Frank Armstrong and Wim Crouwel to name but a few. Unfortunately it is probably the case that these truly talented people are reluctant showmen and women.

Yours sincerely Andrew Pritchard

Reply from the chair
Andrew, watch the diary dates on page 14 you may be pleasantly surprised in the near future.

Dear Freda and David, a brief letter of thanks for organizing the Müller-Brockmann evening last Thursday. It was a great event and much appreciated by everyone from Addison who attended. I can understand how demanding arranging this kind of thing is and I hope you've both been thanked a lot.

Kind regards Phil Rushton

Awards feedback

Dear Freda, dear David
After having spent a nice weekend in London we are now back in Berlin recalling our memories. Congratulations for the pretty good organization and the choice you and the other members of the jury made. Although I suppose you enjoy having finished this deal of work, be assured that all new members. myself included, are looking forward to the society's newsletter.

Yours sincerely Ben Buschfeld

Dear Helen
Thank you very much for your invitation to become a member of the STD. My wife and me are honoured to join the society, so you could list us as new members. The program of the society is very interesting and we are looking forward to hear more about your activities.

Karin & Bertram Schmidt-Friderichs

Dear Mrs Freda Sack
Thank you very much for the invitation to the presentation of the STD TypoGraphic Awards. I feel through the distinction honoured.

Sincerely Gottfried Pott

85

DEMIAN CONRAD: Coming from Switzerland and staying here all week, I've felt the local London vibe so strongly, it's rather strange... I think it's important to leverage the urban aspect of some areas of design. For instance, Tibor Kalman was doing that in New York in the 1990s, and he did it brilliantly.

HOLGER JACOBS: Yes, that's a very important point. I really like it when I travel to some remote region, say go on holiday to Turkey: you roll into a small town on a bus and you see all these billboards with really hideous yet somehow beautiful type advertising local bars, spas or hotels – what you would call vernacular typography. I really like that. My issue with typefaces is that I think there is a general problem with everything becoming generic and too perfect.

I think there's a very relevant, important difference between British design and Swiss design, and possibly even German design. I have a photo that explains it best (page 153). It's a vernacular piece that I feel is a virtual piece of concrete poetry. I think it was taken before my holiday. There's always an 'Oops!' moment, you know? Oops, we messed that up a little bit. Oops, I'm a bit late. Oops, there was some problem on the tube, Oops, bugger, I didn't really think that through. Oops, Brexit, how did that happen? So there is always this potential for things going wrong. It's kind of funny, but it's also pretty scary. I had a Swiss intern who lived in a house at the end of Brick Lane; the house burnt down. She barely survived, she jumped out of the window, she had glass in her face... She showed up at the doorstep of my house at six in the morning; she smelled of smoke and said 'nobody wants to know about this'. The police didn't care; she went to the hospital, they sent her away, so I rang up the council, I rang up everyone and nobody really gave a damn. The policeman just said, 'We have so many cases each day, we can't really look into it' – she only survived by chance. Would it have been any different if she had died? Yes, probably. After I had called everyone I could think of, I rang the Swiss Embassy in London since she was a Swiss citizen. The woman there said 'I was working for the Swiss Consulate in Kolkata, India for ten years and it was so much better and more organised over there, I can't wait until I'm out of this country'. If it had happened in Germany, it would be on the national news, it would be in conversation, there would be assurances, there would be investigations, the whole thing, you know? Here, a lot of things go wrong. However, in terms of design, I think of Switzerland as a pretty organised country. I don't know if that is still true, but when a Swiss friend started working with me here in London, I noticed that he had real issues with the 'oops' mentality: when things went wrong at the printers, he introduced me to that nice Swiss word mängelrüge, a funny Swiss word for a complaint about an error, the type of thing that doesn't generally happen in Switzerland. Here in the UK, if some-one owes you money – you know, clients never pay – it's always a real hassle, invoices always seem to get lost: we used to call it 'dropping the key' – well, you might give their address to someone at Brixton Market, or hire somebody... You can't really take anyone to court. There's small claims court, where you wait forever, or if you take it to a bigger court, the case is basically decided based on who has the most money for the best solicitor. Everything is a mess in England, but it's also a good thing. It's a good sort of mess, a creative mess. You need to learn how to make something out of nothing, nobody has money, rents are ridiculous, so you think a lot in terms of how to produce, or how to compensate for a lack of funds, or all the things that can go wrong in print. You need to know how to do something that is more creative or more inventive, when failure, a misprint, or things like that, are already intrinsic to the process. You make use of cheap materials you can buy at the corner shop or a hardware store, you spray it or turn it on its head and do something different with it to turn it into an interesting design. I find that a lot is based on thinking about production: often you never know if you will actually get paid, nobody wants to pay, your clients do not have much money, it's all a bit dodgy, all a bit difficult. Often you are given a token budget for something. So you wonder how you can produce the project in an original way using the least amount of money. 'I wonder if I can make that kind of production process part of the design?' At least that's how we thought about design at the Royal College. There was a lot of experimentation with materials and processes, without a whiff of Max Bill's Gute Form.

DC: That seems to be quite a different approach to design. So, tell me about what you have brought with you?

HJ: This is Cornel Windlin's programme for Schauspielhaus Zurich (page 97–99). He won the award for most beautiful book, or something like that, and he definitely deserved it. I never really met Cornel. I bumped into him at openings and such, but he probably doesn't know who I am, even though I obviously know who he is. I had someone from Zurich working with me, Marco Müller. He worked with me for a year, then left to go work with Cornel. I knew it would work out for him there, and I couldn't really be very upset with him since it was a very good opportunity for him. I was a bit disappointed that he left me, but he was also one of those really stubborn Swiss guys. In a sense, he wasn't really smooth enough, he wasn't improvising enough for London but he had his own definite ideas and he pushed those through. At any rate, I like this piece because I design identities: visual identities, corporate identities and systems. This was an identity where I initially thought ok, this is not a logo, this is just a dot. You couldn't even register this as a mark. On the other hand, it's so much more than just a dot. It marks a position, a place in Zurich, a certain location. I don't know what Cornel's intention was, but that is how I perceive it. In a sense, it's marking a space in the city, in society. It's also a mirror in a sense: I mean the way this programme works, it features scenes from daily life in Zurich. It's oddly 'off the grid', which I really like. I think he overprinted the sheets over and over again: that's very much an idea I can identify with, it's just the way it was printed. It's somehow very 'London-like'. It has this interesting effect that's hard to define, it looks like they recycled those left-over sheets which printers often use for getting the registration right. In a way, they seem to have come off the press haphazardly. They are just happening. They are more or less accidental images, snapshots of what's going on in the moment that were produced before Instagram, social media and all that. I don't know when exactly, around 2010. It's a very immediate, somehow honest impression. I think he got criticised for that because he showed those drunk guys and creepy people – basically, he shows a little bit too much of the dark side of Zurich. I like the thin paper, like a phone directory. It's a little bit grubby, quite punk even. Even so, the thing that I find most interesting is the logo, or the non-logo. I have thought a lot about that. I think what interests me most about logo design, identity design, is not the actual design, but rather dealing with the clients, seeing how they think about things: how they struggle with this, how they want to coalesce all their values, all their meaning, everything that matters to them, into some sort of simple icon, a little jewel, some sort of small mark that is charged with so much meaning and power, but this is just a dot, in a way it says, ok, forget about all that, there is real life out there, it's not like this condensed experience that we call design. This continues to fascinate me. It fits quite well into my perceptions about identity, whether it be general or corporate identities, because I've tried for many years to get rid of logos or turn logos into more playful systems, almost devaluing them in a way, in order to say, 'hey, there are other things out there'. I think this focus on logos has a lot to do with unconscious religious ideas that we still carry with us, because in the end it's all about one's values, one's view of the world – that's a lot to condense into one central idea, or one central meaning.

This is a Japanese Shinto spirit, called a *Kami* (page 96). It's obviously some cute little thing from Studio Ghibli, they call them *Makkuro kurosuke*, basically little bits of dust, little living dust flakes. However they really symbolise a kami, a sort of spirit. Shintoism is a nature-based religion where spiritual presence is perceived as residing in everything: the trees, the wind, movement, stones, water. When we go to say, a Catholic church, there's this big cross right in the middle of it, you can't miss it, it's a sort of super logo. When you go to a Shinto shrine, there is nothing but a piece of cloth waving in the wind. Its movement indicates some sort of presence, and that's what this logo is, a presence you can't ignore. Its significance is far wider, its meaning is not centralised or compressed into one icon, it's actually everything around it, and it's also what's hidden behind it. I find that piece of work truly impressive. Perhaps I see more in it than Cornel intended.

You were asking me what I find significant about Swiss design. There is a real element of craftsmanship required to create things that are that clear and that simple, as you say, a kind of Müller-Brockmann way of doing things. I often tell my students that they can always do something that looks experimental, expressive or messy, even a bit punk, but in the end, it's all about hygiene. I don't say, 'come and learn the rules'. Instead I say, 'look, I'm not interested in teaching typographic rules, I just expect a bit of personal hygiene: you get up in the morning and brush your teeth, maybe take a shower, put on a fresh pair of underpants. That kind of stuff. It's the same thing with graphic design – you should know how to do decent kerning, you should know which hyphens to use, you should know the basics of typography. From that perspective you can quickly tell if a piece of work was done by someone who actually knows his craft, or if it was done by an amateur who just happened by sheer luck to produce something really interesting. With a Poster that looks funky at first sight, you just need to look at the hyphens or how the dates and the address are set and know immediately if it's done by someone who knows what they are doing, or if it's just a happy accident.

DC: When you came to London at the beginning of your career, were there other people from Switzerland with whom you connected?

HJ: No, I started out in London first and then I went to Japan. I came back and then, for a couple of years, I wasn't really doing much of interest, just trying to get by and pay the rent. I was mostly designing books because I had been working for a book publisher in Japan and I had brought some work home with me and had continued to work freelance for them, but they weren't great books. They were just ok. They weren't books you would see in an art bookshop. Anyway, then I started doing work that was a bit more varied, more interesting, and suddenly someone applied for an internship: Cornelia Müller. I think she has a design studio in Lucerne now. She was my first contact with another Swiss designer in the UK. She was a very good designer, she really knew her craft, but wasn't stiff about it. So I worked with her for a bit, and then a friend of hers came along: Marco [Müller], who had graduated from Zurich University of the Arts (ZHdK). He wanted to come to London and work with me. He ended up becoming my first proper paid employee. It wasn't easy, he was a very stubborn guy but he remains a good friend of mine; I respect him. He is also a very good designer. However, I think if you really want to take on a project completely, and make your mark, you need to have lived in London for a little while to understand how this city works. All the more so if you are working in a commercial or semi-commercial environment and you design brands. You need to check out other brands, see what the competition is like. I remember one situation: we designed something for this jewellery arts label and he [Marco] came up with a design that had a lot of stripes. I immediately said that it looked like something for Paul Smith. Everyone knows Paul Smith in London. It's a major British brand.

However, Marco didn't consider it to be a problem. I kept insisting that we could not show it because it looked too 'Paul Smith'. So, there we were at the presentation, and the first thing the client said was, 'that's Paul Smith'! There were a lot of incidents like that. We worked well together, then Marco left to work for Cornel. After that, I had a few other Swiss who came to work as interns and went on to become employees or collaborators. For instance, I worked with Andy Lang for a long time – three, four, five years. All of them came from the same place: Zurich University of the Arts (ZHdK). They were very different designers, but they were all very good in their own individual way.

DC: Would you say that England went from the William Morris Arts and Crafts era, with its wallpaper and centred text, to the modern era of Jan Tschichold, with its sleek, minimalistic design?

HJ: Not exactly: they never really became very clean, or modernist. Nowadays there is a trend in British design that is heavily influenced by modernist Swiss design. Many of the design studios working along these lines are from the north of England. One is actually called North and quite a few other design studios are following in their footsteps. They basically do what they would probably refer to as 'timeless design'. When I was studying in the 1990s, everyone was playing with this deconstruction thing, sort of messing about with type on the photocopier. At Central Saint Martins, sometimes there was a queue so long it would take two hours to get to the photocopier. We would move a sheet with type while copying and make it look really messy. I remember David Carson coming over to the Saint Martins show on a recruitment tour. It's probably similar to what is happening now, everyone was following a trend. These were the top schools, Saint Martins, and the RCA: people were doing something similar there, maybe with a bit more concept and a bit more thinking behind it. However, this was not what clients were looking for at the time. It was not really about providing solutions. More like creating more problems, or questioning the process. Consequently, there was really a good niche for the studios that followed this very clean 1950s and 1960s Swiss style, and they became incredibly successful. They had no competition since everyone else was doing messy experimental stuff that doesn't really work in practice. Once they became very successful, students also began to adopt their style. I remember going to a degree show, I think it was at the London College of Communication; I went into the show and thought 'wow, this all looks so good and so proper', I walked around and then I realised hey, hold on, this is all set in Helvetica Bold. A degree show and every project was set in Helvetica Bold – I guess that's kind of where things went in two different directions. There's a lot of London design that's very modernist; they look at the Schweizer Typografische Monatsblätter, and they modernise that style a little bit. Maybe the colours are a little bit fresher, and there is a hint of fun in it, but it's essentially the Swiss design of the 1950s and 1960s. Then there is a whole other school of thought that is far more interested in experimentation, slightly odd stuff, process, and quirky materials. I think that, generally speaking, the British like a bit of kitsch. They like their doilies, their little knitted things, their tea cosies and cluttered little Victorian houses. I think that's very much part of the British mentality.

As a result, I would say you have two different poles. the North, with its very clean, very modernist look, definitely harkening back to Switzerland. Then you have Graphic Through Facilities, I see them as very much in the British tradition of Alan Fletcher, very experimental, very playful, very unpredictable, you never really know what they will do next, but it's always good, so I have great respect for them.

Graphic design from the modernist era always works, that is also the dangerous thing about it. It works for everything. There is one good example of Swiss design by Fridolin Müller for Ciba-Geigy: I think it was for some sort itching and allergy medication. There is another Swiss design by Emil Ruder for an exhibition of modern French rugs at the Museum für Gestaltung. When you put them next to each other, they look exactly the same. The same design, the same colours, the same typeface for an allergy medication and a cultural exhibition. What's worse, both work, both are fine. It kind of works for everything. It works for every regime as well. You can use it for right-wing, for left-wing, for capitalism, for communism... You really can use it for anything. I think that's what Tschichold had problems with. It's so functional, yet still creative.

DC: What emerged in our previous conversation was that the purpose of Swiss typography was to solve the problem of legibility. Consequently it's really easy to read, and its methodology and structure are made with the aim of conveying a maximum of informtion as quickly as possible. Of course, it could work for everything. However, there is something quite odd going on in Switzerland, a revival of sorts of the Swiss style. It's not only about the methodology, although we are almost all using it to solve problems, but I would say there is a kind of styled revivalism. What do you think?

HJ: Look at what Experimental Jetset is doing in the Netherlands: they use a palette of simple colours, and one typeface, maybe two, and they can create so many variations with that. It always impresses me; you think it's all been done. You wonder how much you can do with a few bars, lines, two or three typefaces, and a simplified colour palette. Then you look at the work of Experimental Jetset and they've got it, there is still so much in it and what's more, there is a real focus on content as well. It's not just stylistic messing about and rearranging things. You really do have to focus on content. As a result, it still looks fresh and new. You don't look at it and think, 'that's from the 1960s', although you can see where the influence comes from; it's something beyond, post-Swiss graphic design.

I recently met Veronica Fuerte from Hey Studio in Barcelona. Her work is very colourful, she likes these bright colours, it's sunny in Barcelona. If you ask her about her influences – you can also see it in her work – it's definitely Swiss design. I would say it is some sort of Spanish or Catalan interpretation of the Swiss design of the 1960s, and it works very well. I think what I envy about designers from that period is their use of a limited palette. It actually spurs one to think much bigger, because you are less distracted by all the possibilities. Sometimes I wish I could go back in time and do that kind of thing. Delete all the typefaces from my computer, except for three, then choose six, seven colours and see how much I can get out of that more simplified palette.

DC: Can you name some similarities you have observed between Swiss and British culture?

HJ: That's a difficult one isn't it? I think Swiss design is organised and structured and the British obviously rebelled against that. So a lot of later Swiss design is quite rough, really breaking all the rules. Something similar has been happening in England, but more directly inspired by the Punk movement. However, perhaps it was for different reasons, for different motivations. Perhaps it's more because everything really is quite rough in London because of poverty, bad politics, Margaret Thatcher and all that. In Switzerland perhaps things developed in a certain way because everything was far too cosy and 'gemütlich'. I think that's the same thing that annoys me. I don't know, in Germany, you always get the urge to cause a bit of trouble, say on the tube, or on the bus, I would really like to take my clothes off and do something freaky. People would react to that, they would be scared, they would say 'ah, there's a freaky person'. In England, if you did that on the tube, everyone would just stare at their newspaper, thinking 'ok, there's goes another one, I'm just going to try not to notice him': it has no effect. That's the good and the bad thing about this country, like Germany. You can actually cause a bit of trouble there, which is very hard in England. Very hard. It's really hard to find similarities.

DC: In Zurich people are always a little bit afraid of Germans because they are so direct.

HJ: If that's true then it's an interesting point, since that's very British. They never really say exactly what they mean: if you hear 'well, there's some sort of interesting idea in it, we might consider it, this really has potential...' in plain English it really means, 'that's rubbish, it's in the bin already, fuck off and never bother me again!' When you run into someone and say 'it's so nice bumping into you, let's get together for lunch sometime' you know that means, 'it was a bit embarrassing meeting you like this, I hope we never meet again'. It's sort of a fluffy language. It's not like that in Germany. In Germany you say very clearly what you want, to the point of sounding a bit insulting. It's also annoying for me as a German, I came to study here at the Royal College of Art, and I didn't know what the hell they were talking about because I had studied in Germany before and criticism was very clear and hard. For that reason, it doesn't really work. Here they would never have this kind of clear discussion. However, you need to learn to read between the lines and now I actually like it. It's much more work in English – an email is probably three times longer because there's a lot of fluff: 'maybe', and 'could be', 'we should consider'... all that sort of thing, but I like it. It's very Japanese in a way. Now you're telling me it's very Swiss, fine, there you go. When I deal with American clients, I find them very hard, very scary. They are always like, 'make this logo 20% bigger and move it 3 mm up' and I think 'ok, I'll just do that'. Then, on second thought I wonder 'who is the designer here who studied this stuff for years and years, me or you?' and then I think, 'is it actually worth arguing about it?' The answer is probably not. Not with Americans.

es rächts...
es runds...
es Hürlimaa

Hürlimann Bier

das runde Bier

98

Schau Spiel Haus Zürich 2009/10

Michele Jannuzzi

DEMIAN CONRAD: We already have some things in common: both of us are from Ticino, a minority canton, and we are also both Swiss designers who work abroad. What objects have you brought here?

MICHELE JANNUZZI: I have a few objects to show you: here is something by Max Huber (page 110-111), because he is Swiss, and yet he's a very 'un-Swiss' designer. I am not Swiss, I am Italian, by culture and, in a way, by identity. Max Huber, a pioneer and master of graphic design, made his career in Italy and, although I am far from being on his level, I do feel some points of similarity with him. I also have a personal link to Huber, since I was a student of his during the last year he taught. I actually had personal contact with him while studying in Lugano; I remember, at the time, he was living in Arzo (TI) with his wife. I was a first-year graphic design student, and, at that point, he was quite old, and just about to retire, he was about sixty-four – he had trouble moving about. He was short, smaller than I was. There we were in our classroom, waiting for Huber to turn up – everyone was chatting about what an important graphic designer he was, that we were very lucky to have him and so on, and this guy comes in, almost in slow motion, not even acknowledging that we were in the room. He comes into the room and heads for the wastebasket. He begins to rummage through it, again very, very slowly, like one of those lumbering slow animals, in slow motion, sifting through stuff. Then, clutching a little piece of paper, he straightens up and says in his heavy smoker's voice, *'guardate quanti pezzi di colore buttate via'* [look how many bits of colour you are throwing away]. My other object is the iconic Fixpencil, manufactured by Caran d'Ache. It is like the pen in *2001: A Space Odyssey* by Stanley Kubrick.

That is the way you achieve things – that is important to me. There was another seminal book that I considered bringing along, *Designing Programmes* by Karl Gerstner, but I decided to leave it behind. Gerstner influenced my understanding of what constitutes Swiss graphic design. In that book he proposes, in a roundabout scientific way, a means by which we can actually simplify and improve the world, but there is not as much of a personal attachment.

There was also another option, I could have brought my wife. My wife is Swiss; I am the son of Italian immigrants who arrived in Switzerland when I was very small, so, while I grew up in Switzerland – all my childhood and youth was spent there – in a sense, I always lived in a sort of Italian bubble, sheltered from many influences. Even the ones we experienced appeared as distinctively alien. Basically, my extended family back in Italy didn't eat fondue, it appeared to be a sort of exotic thing. My family didn't really 'get' spätzle: we liked it, and I ate plenty of spätzle in my youth – but it was a sort of alien thing. For me, living with my wife was actually my first real experience of 'Swissness' in my home. Then I began to experience life and things that came from Switzerland, not as an external experience, but as part and parcel of my life.

DC: You and Richard Smith are probably among the rare British-Swiss graphic design couples that I know of who are working together here in London.

MJ: In the UK, even. One parallel I could cite is Minale-Tattersfield. However, Marcello [Minale] was Italian, and Brian [Tattersfield] is British, and both of them attended the RCA so there was a rapprochement in that sense. Since I sound Italian, and I have an Italian name, this parallel was somehow established. Most people don't realize that Italian culture is part of Swiss culture. Here in London, people assume that Swiss are either of German or French background. Some realise there are Italians, but pretty much no one realises that there are Romansch as well.

DC: What prompted you to come to London?

MJ: When I finished my studies at CSIA (Centro Scolastico per le Industrie Artistiche), I began working for Francesco Milani at a studio in Giubiasco – we are still in touch. I just saw him at his home to celebrate his 80th birthday, and his son works with me here in London. My intent at the time was to work so I could save up and continue my studies – I wanted more time to discover more things. For me, CSIA was an extraordinary place – I know that people are not always complimentary about it but I thought it was phenomenally good. They had really small classes, taught by really extraordinary people, like Huber, along with Serge Libiszewski, Felix Burkard and Bruno Monguzzi, to name but a few, as well as the less well-known Lulo Tognola and Emilio Rissone, all of whom had quite an influence on us. Our class was a tiny group, only six or seven people. Now the class I teach in Madrid contains forty students.

So, I wanted to study somewhere, and I examined different options. I looked at Basel and Zurich, I looked at France – there was a school in Paris that appealed to me, as well as other places like the Pasadena Art Center in Vevey. Then a friend of mine said that I should check out the RCA. I wrote a letter requesting information, and one day I got a big parcel from the UK with a catalogue, a prospectus, a couple of bits inside, enough to learn about people like Gert Dumbar, Derek Birdsall and Alan Kitching, and other names I didn't yet know. I quickly researched them and I very much liked their experimental approach. At that point, the RCA was the most experimental place of the lot. The ArtCenter also promoted itself as experimental but I felt it was more marketing oriented; my feeling was that the RCA came off as more genuine. I took a cheap flight and went to visit. I knocked on the door and Paul Neale of GTF (Graphic Thought Facility) opened the door and showed me around; he was in his first year. Paul must have been the first person I met in London, it's funny that, thirty years later, we ended up living a few steps away from each other. At the time the RCA was still at 24 Kensington Court. A family ambiance reigned inside; we were a family of graphic designers, so it was in a sense the ultimate, ideal set-up. It was also a kind of natural continuation of my CSIA experience, although it was a totally different environment with different cultural influences – the stimulus I was receiving was very new to me.

DC: Were there other Swiss people coming to London then?

MJ: I should look at the graduation list, but I don't believe there was a single Swiss in any of the departments. If there had been someone, they must have been Italian. There were many students from all over the world. I remember there were many Italians, they formed a large portion of the foreign student community. I may be wrong but I think I was the only Swiss there. At the time, when I talked among peers in Switzerland, no one mentioned the Royal College of Art, although *Graphis* did a special issue [no. 146] in the 1970s showcasing both the Basel School of Design and the Royal College of Art. Walter Herdeg, the editor of *Graphis*, said he picked the two colleges because they embodied an 'essential dichotomy of modern art education'. It featured a cover by Richard Guyatt, a presentation of the Royal College of Art. I made it my business to get hold of it. It was a sheet of millimetre paper, with three little objects, a small head, a stone heart and a hand. So, the RCA was known in the Swiss design community, but there was not much talk about it.

DC: When you came to London, did you bring some of the Swiss design discipline or methodologies with you, such as the use of grids, readable typesetting, and Akzidenz-Grotesk?

MJ: Swiss design was a known entity. In the 1970s, an important period in the UK, Dennis Bailey was working for *Graphis* in Zurich. When he returned to the UK, he brought along the Swiss International Style. In the 1980s, groups like Octavo were followers of Wolfgang Weingart. The Basel School became popular and fashionable in the British design community. So Swiss design was well-known, but, while in Switzerland it was accepted as dogma, when I arrived in the UK, everyone was trying to create their own version of it. Groups like Why Not Associates, who were at the RCA before me, were at the forefront of people who were questioning British design. Their agency was aptly named: if you went over and asked them why they were doing something, they would reply, 'why not?'

DC: Have you encountered designers who were critical of Swiss typography?

MJ: In the UK, people like Herbert Spencer and Anthony Froshaug were peers of Josef Müller-Brockmann and Karl Gerstner in terms of their approach to design. They were very close, and they were true modernists. However, the sort of modernist period we experienced in Switzerland did not really happen in the UK. After the Second World War, in the 1950s and 1960s, the modernism that we saw in Switzerland took the form of the Pop Art movement in the UK. It was far more exciting, faster, colourful and so on. In Switzerland, Pop Art never quite rivalled the modernist thinking of the 1920s and 1930s, which continued to carry on into the 1950s and 1960s. In the 1970s, there was the International Style in the UK, which came from Switzerland via America, and, in the 1980s, groups like Octavo or Why Not Associates were inspired by Wolfgang Weingart, whom you could almost categorise as a Dutch designer even though he is Swiss, and who remains a central figure of Swiss design. In the same way, Huber and Monguzzi perpetuated Swiss design, albeit in Italy. Other countries began adopting the style associated with Swiss design. I think it still carries on, it has not disappeared, and it provides an efficient solution to many problems, so they used it as a point of departure, and this has continued on for decades.

DC: The exchange of culture is sometimes about love and hate, attraction and rejection, friendship and partnership. Do you think UK design culture influenced the Swiss design scene?

MJ: I do believe it has. A lot of Swiss designers spent time in London, especially in the 1990s and the 2000s. The capital is a cultural point of reference for many people. So yes, the 1990s onwards was seen as a period when more interesting things were happening. This attracted a lot of attention and people started taking notice: figures like Neville Brody, Tomato, Why Not – there was a definite influence. I felt that the interest amongst my peers at the RCA did not consist of a knowledge of Swiss graphic design from a logical standpoint, rather they connected with it in terms of style. To return to my explanation of modernist principles: the original proposition of figures such as Gerstner and Müller-Brockmann was not about a style; there was indeed an inherent style, but it was not so much an aesthetic choice as much as an aesthetic generated by the problems they were confronting. A number of useful conversations took place amongst people like Richard [Smith] and myself, as well as others, all of which resulted in our taking a closer look at the work of Froshaug and Spencer. We were also fortunate to have Alan Kitching as a tutor; he was closely connected with Froshaug.

DC: Swiss design was disseminated in European design communities through such vehicles as *Graphis* and *Neue Grafik*. In your opinion, by what means did the British and, more specifically, London design communities, extend their influence in the world?

MJ: I think Neville Brody played a key role in that respect through things like *Fuse* magazine and the Victoria and Albert museum exhibition *The Language of Neville Brody*. This exhibition was probably the largest and most important graphic design exhibition ever mounted, and the one that has had the largest impact – an impact, in my opinion, that has been unequalled either before or since. I don't wish to be dismissive by any means, but I think the exhibition was even bigger than Brody himself. It was held at the V&A in 1988, and went on to tour around the world. Anybody who was anybody in graphic design – whether in Switzerland or anywhere else in the west – knew about the catalogue of that exhibition, whether they liked it or not. I remember speaking to Milani, who knew about it, but dismissed it, saying that it was all déjà vu, nothing new. He felt it was a rehashing of Dadaism, merely cobbling together a number of influences and offering it up as a style.

The reason it was so important is that I think Brody made graphic design into a discipline that was relevant, cool, desirable and socially engaged. When I started out in graphic design, I didn't know who the hell Brody was. However, by the time I graduated, Brody was out there, making me and what I do a little bit cooler than it would otherwise be, because he popularised our profession and made it attractive. So the exhibition was important for that reason. However, if I were to just look specifically at the work itself, I would say that Brody's work will probably not stand the test of time, and endure in the same ways was that of Müller-Brockmann.

DC: I think in Switzerland, companies such as Geigy and Swissair, along with the national rail networks, were propagating the image of this Swiss methodology and style. On the other hand, during the 1990s, British magazines, such as *Arena* and *Face*, were also quite influential abroad.

MJ: At some point, Swiss designers began to reject the dogma, giving rise to a new generation that was able to do different things, able to appreciate Brody. What happened in the UK in the 1980s and 1990s began to happen in Switzerland in the 1990s and 2000s. There are many good examples of great stuff, and some extraordinary ones such as Cornel Windlin, but overall, my perception is that there was a rejection of the dogma and a major lack of ambition in terms of what the Swiss were doing. Some years ago, there was an exhibition in Zurich entitled *100 Years of Swiss Graphic Design* at the Museum für Gestaltung Zürich. I spent some time at it, and I perceived a lack of ambition that I did not see in the UK. The *Neue Grafik* crowd, Müller-Brockmann, Hans Neuburg, Gerstner and Carlo Vivarelli, were all using graphic design as a way to change society at large, and, in that respect, Brody's work was informed by similar principles. His use of magazines provided a means of reach-ing many people, and enabled him to disseminate his visual approach in a very effective way. When the Swiss were designing brand identities for everything from airlines [Swissair] to electric appliances, such as Electrolux, they were creating the future. That generation, in Switzerland as well as in the UK, were able to propagate their work in a manner that affected society at large. The impression the Zurich exhibition left on me was that my contemporaries were creating a sort of 'niche' graphic design, i.e. designing for graphic designers. The exhibition showed the great Swiss graphic designers who had been working on airlines turning to projects such as the designing of posters or leaflets for 'niche' events. There was a lot of visual excitement around all that, but no real underlying ambition to leverage it, like going to a large corporation, and saying, 'Look! I can make this for you!'

DC: That is so true. In 2002, when André Dosé took over Swissair, he hired Tyler Brûlé to redesign the identity and the typeface was designed by Freda Sack. It was a project designed by British designers but the result looks so Swiss and modernist.

MJ: Indeed, but, in point of fact, they recently rebranded it. You might say that Brûlé got the style right, but the visual identity did not stand the test of time. The end result was that they removed the two blocks, and went back to the drawing board to develop something more functional.

DC: I have a feeling that, here in Switzerland, subsequent generations will return to the traditions of the Swiss International Style. For instance, Swiss Typefaces released the Swiss typeface, Optimo in Geneva released Theinhardt Grotesk and Lineto Unica77.

MJ: There was a time when I was very engaged with all the changes and what was going on. I see things and I look with interest at things I like. In Switzerland, I see good quality design in many places: I think the educational system in Switzerland is still effective in terms of teaching good graphic design, which might not always be the case here in the UK. Nevertheless, I have perceived a return to what I would refer to as more modernist principles. I don't know if it is a natural move or similar to the revival one saw in the 1970s. I see people in the graphic design community who delve into the history, searching for something more significant than simply the style. We have one client in Lausanne for whom we do quite a lot of work, the Cinémathèque Suisse. We created their identity, signage, posters, programmes, and the design style we use for them is very Swiss, very typographic, however there is a hint of a challenge to it, perhaps you could qualify it as a British element. People praise us for including elements amounting to a Swiss revival, and we have seen that it is very popular with students. There must be some visual popularity regarding that type of thing, of which we did had not been intentionally aware. When we redesigned the brand, we thought that for such a classic institution their identity needed to be rooted in the history and heritage of those who had preceded us, such as Werner Jeker. We felt the need to seek a continuity with that. Consequently, our aim was to design the brand to look as if it had always been like that. It had been different – actually, we made a total break from what they had done before, but it was made to look as if it was a retro, traditional type of brand. For a different organisation we would have wanted a total break from the past, but for Cinémathèque Suisse we wanted a timeless sort of brand. We did not expect it to become so popular with young people.

DC: My last question concerns Gerstner and his ideas in *Designing Programmes*. How has that influenced your practice?

MJ: In my view, Gerstner lives on. His book, *Designing Programmes*, is still relevant, because the approach from a time when mechanisation was increasingly used to create pages remains the same – you have to find ways, such as a grid or a system, to streamline the process of creating pages, in a way that stresses unity, uniformity, consistency and so on. The same currently applies to the increasing automation of the electronic world. It is true that, in a lot of the work Richard [Smith] and I both do, we continue to preserve and value our typographic modernist training with great pride, which we owe to Froshaug and Gerstner. If you can design a system, you can create quality in a far more effective and efficient way. We were experimenting with this for many years. Then, in the late 1990s, we were commissioned to design marketing materials for Central Saint Martins [University of the Arts, London], our first really large-scale project. At the time, a website was not considered to be as important as it is today, and you had to accomplish miracles with virtually nothing, nevertheless, we had been allotted quite a substantial print budget, since the catalogue was still being sent out to thousands of prospective students. By creating a system to merge the two, we were able to produce both for print, and for the Web. This was highly advantageous since we were able to design a database driven programme in a very time-efficient manner, extending the marketing time for all curricula. The College was developing part-time courses with a very short shelf-life to be offered during the Christmas and Summer breaks and they had to get that information out as soon as possible to maximise the number of students. We were able to streamline the process and still produce something that was intensely designed, and up to the requirements of an institution like Central Saint Martins. They gained two extra weeks in which to market their courses. It was all about recognising a business need and optimising our use of the available technology. We went on to apply this everywhere. Regarding the case I mentioned before – namely the programme for Cinémathèque Suisse – everyone thinks it's highly designed, but the pages were actually produced in a matter of seconds, because the system was designed to address 99% of the requirements. Currently, we mainly work on InDesign, but we started out on Quark Xpress. At the moment, we are producing design software for a large engineering company. They are engineers, so they love this, but even for them, it's still very surprising. You might argue that we are cutting ourselves out of a job, but I don't think that is the case. I think we should embrace automation. This is why Gerstner remains so relevant, because otherwise you are left with two options: you either structure yourself into a little niche, where the craft model you mentioned before is sufficient. Or you seek to have a more mainstream impact. Then you need to equip yourself differently: that is the lesson taught by Gerstner, Müller-Brockmann and Froshaug. It is still very relevant because unfortunately, too much marketing and design today is in the hands of very average people. Designers working in a small bubble should have more ambition and channel their creativity for a wider public. I am not saying that it is an easy thing to do, but I believe it will be a better world if we all try to reach out instead of simply living in a nutshell.

max huber
progetti grafici 1936_1981

elect

Richard Hollis

DEMIAN CONRAD: Thank you for coming to the gallery here in Brick Lane. Can you begin with your introduction to Swiss graphic design?

RICHARD HOLLIS: I got involved with Swiss graphic design through my interest in Swiss concrete art. I had begun working as a graphic designer at the same time as I was making these vaguely mathematical sort of paintings based on simple geometry, a bit like the work of Richard Paul Lohse. In those days you earned a lot of money, relatively speaking, so you could afford to work on just one job, because there were hardly any graphic designers around. Consequently the graphic design scene in London was a small world and we all knew each other pretty well.

I had done a job for what was then the nationalised British Iron and Steel Federation, which was represented in the British pavilion at the Brussels World Expo in 1958. I don't know how I got that particular job; it was an illustrated catalogue of films on steelmaking. I travelled to Brussels and I finished up my trip to the Continent at the Venice Biennale, partly because I was interested in Venezuelan geometrical abstract painting, with its machine-made look. On my way south, I went to see Lohse in Zurich. He was very generous with me, we discussed his paintings and he told me that, if I was interested in graphic design, that I should go see Josef Müller-Brockmann, a very influential designer. So, I went to the Kunstgewerbeschule: back then, Müller-Brockmann was head of the department, and he showed me around. Quite by chance there was an exhibition on Henry Van de Velde (I wrote a book on him later) for which JMB had done a poster. Müller-Brockmann was one of the editors of the magazine *Neue Grafik*, which I had already seen in the library at what was then the London School of Printing and Graphic Arts [now the London College of Communication]. Many of us teaching there were interested and excited by *Neue Grafik*. From the moment it came out, I was an unconditional fan and remain so, and then I actually was able to meet its editor [Lohse]. I was lucky enough to have met two of the editors of *Neue Grafik* in its heyday.

In London we were all interested in what was happening in Swiss design, especially Ken Garland. He was working for a magazine here called *Design*, which was very poorly printed, and not very interesting at the time. He wanted to find out how it was that *Neue Grafik* was so well done, so he toured around, and went to check out various people in Switzerland. I think he's the first person I'm aware of who actually spent time going around Switzerland to meet people involved with print.

DC: At the time you would have had to go by train to Switzerland, so it was quite a long journey?

RH: Yes, it was, but the trains were very good (page 124). It was before air travel became so easy. However, throughout the second half of the 19th century, and the 20th, rail travel was good, exciting and interesting. In fact, I would say that the avant-garde movement of the 1920s and early 1930s was really made possible by rail travel and personal contacts. One example is the pioneer El Lissitzky who came from Russia, who often spent time in Berlin, by way of the Netherlands and Switzerland. People were travelling a great deal back then. Train travel is actually very easy, in a sense it's easier and more direct than going by air, and the trains were often just as quick. In terms of going to see people in Switzerland, because of our interest, in 1960, I went to Ulm via Zurich with a friend. I remember that, in Zurich, we wanted to meet Mary Vieira, a sculptor who had also done some rather fine posters, but she was away so we ended up spending time with her husband, Carlo Belloli, who published a history of Italian graphic design in *Neue Grafik*. The next person I met with was Siegfried Odermatt, who was both a brilliant typographer, and a great exponent of photographic images. These people were so kind and helpful, and they were happy to give us examples of their work. I saw Odermatt more than once, and we exchanged posters from our collections. I never saw Müller-Brockmann again, even though he did come to London in the 1990s.

It's very difficult to explain just how different Swiss graphic design was from British graphic design. In England, graphic design was done more or less intuitively and there was a greater influence from America.

Despite all that, politically speaking in the UK, we tended to be rather anti-American, and even leftist. You might say that the Swiss were also caught in the middle of the Cold War between Russia and the West. Of course, even as we admired some of their designers, our friends and colleagues were inclined to see Americans as advanced capitalists and, while there was no real Green movement to speak of, obviously we tended toward that critical direction. Ken Garland was one such example of this viewpoint; it was because of people like him that I became interested in the campaign for nuclear disarmament.

DC: What did you learn from your visits to Müller-Brockmann?

RH: Well, Müller-Brockmann wrote this book, *The Graphic Artist and His Design Problems*, which was very influential. At one point, I heard him speak at a conference in Zurich in 1964: they introduced him as Müller-Blockhaus. He was also an illustrator, influenced by the École de Paris, and then he changed his style after seeing people like Lohse and Hans Neuburg, who were doing much more Constructivist stuff. So he altered his style: he had a terrific facility as an illustrator, with a style reminiscent of Picasso. He began to do exhibition design, which you might fairly call modernist. If you think of the traditional Swiss design of *Neue Grafik* magazine, which was more Constructivist, you could call him modernist. He had begun to get a bit more modern, and move away from his more subjective work in illustration. People like Siegfried Odermatt were very different because they seem to have sprung straight up out of the *Neue Grafik* sphere. Quite a few of the Basel people came to Zurich, very talented people, including Nelly Rudin, for example, who worked with Müller-Brockmann and was also a concrete artist. The most influential person as far as I was concerned was actually Karl Gerstner. I met him in 1964, during the Swiss National Exhibition in Lausanne. He was also a concrete artist, as well as a superbly inventive designer and typographer, an historian of the subject and a serious theorist. It's also why I brought his book today [Gerstner's book *Designing Programmes*] to show you (page 122), because it was extraordinarily influential. Also, it was published by Alec Tiranti, whose bookshop was very close to where I used to live in Central London. Back in the day, many of us frequented Alec Tiranti's bookshop. By the way, Nina Paim, a researcher at the Hochschule der Künste in Bern, who was writing about Gerstner's publisher, Niggli, came to see me in London a few years ago. She was enquiring about Tiranti, and I told her that he wasn't so much a publisher – his bookshop was also a place where sculptors and model makers could buy tools. In addition, for many of us, the architectural magazines at Tiranti's book-shop were an important influence. It was one of the only shops that sold magazines from the Continent, almost the only place where we could see Swiss magazines such as *Werk* and *Bauen und Wohnen*. It was through them that I subscribed to Marcel Wyss's *Spirale*. It was at Tiranti's that we learned that there was another possible path for graphic design.

I honestly don't know when or how I first became interested in Swiss design. When I did the catalogue for the British Iron and Steel Federation in 1958, I wanted to use Akzidenz-Grotesk, but instead I used Monotype Grotesque, referred to as Series 215, because it was the nearest thing we had to the Berthold Grotesk. You could have all types of characters made or supplied, like an 'R' with a leg that was completely straight and not curved. I think I changed one or two other letters, and you could order those from a foundry in Wales. In a sense, you could say we tried to make it as Swiss as possible. At the time it seemed to be a new way of doing things, because Switzerland was not seen as the place where cuckoo clocks came from, but rather it was associated with precision and efficiency.

DC: When you began using some of these ideas and design strategies in London, how did your peers and colleagues react?

RH: Well, several people of my generation were inspired by Swiss ideas and design. There was one designer, the late Dennis Bailey, who had worked for *Graphis* magazine in Zurich. When he returned to England, his designs were totally Swiss. I think it would have been in the 1960s that Ken Briggs did a lot of posters for the National Theatre here, as well as programmes. It was more like the Swiss National Theatre than it was like our National Theatre. Briggs died in 2013, but there is a younger colleague here in the UK [Fraser Muggeridge], who produced a small book, nicely illustrated with Briggs's work. Briggs trained as a printer, learning to print like Swiss printers so that the darks in half-tones were actually more or less solid black, in order to create more contrast. That was one of the influences from Swiss design.

DC: When I was speaking with Robin Kinross, he mentioned that, as Londoners, you really admired the printing techniques practiced in Switzerland. What were the differences between printing here in the UK and printing in Switzerland?

RH: I should have brought along a copy of the government-sponsored magazine that Ken Garland had worked for, *Design*. It was the quality of printing that had motivated him to go looking around Switzerland to find out why your printing was so much better. He did write a long report, which I think I probably still have, about his visit to Switzerland. It would be useful for you to have, I doubt even he's got a copy. I think he went to two or three printers, as well as Cliché Schwitter AG, a photo-engraver for whom Gerstner did an advertisement. Technically speaking, the Swiss were better. Also, they had a much wider range of typefaces. For instance, there was a kind of Akzidenz-Grotesk Schmal – there was nothing like it here. At the London School of Printing, there was a teacher who got the students to make a typeface for the company Letraset that was a complete imitation of it. I would say one of the significant things about *Neue Grafik* was that they were interested in the history of graphic design. Indeed, there was Müller-Brockmann's book *The History of Visual Communication*, which did take a look back to see how things had developed from a style standpoint. However, there was no sophisticated analysis of how change happened, no discussion, for example, of the whole notion of the revival of styles or anything like that. That was eventually followed up, in the late 1960s, even 1970s, by *Typografische Monatsblätter*.

There was a sort of standardisation of approach that prevailed until Wolfgang Weingart came along. That was a different sort of influence, with typography and text that was more intellectualised, but his was also a visual influence – his typographic designs were quite exciting. I corresponded with him, and met him on several occasions; I even stayed with him in Basel.

Another instance of direct connection: Karl Gerstner gave me a piece of calligraphy he had done as a student, which was absolutely remarkable. It was not the sort of thing that would have ever been done here in London, at least not in the last fifty years.

When I arrived in Zurich in 1958, I was astonished to see JMB's vast Turmac advertising billboards with black and white photography, set in Akzidenz-Grotesk, in the train station. You couldn't find such a thing in any other country. So, it was like living in a different graphic world. Swiss training was so completely different, I was astonished when I went to the Kunstgewerbeschule in Zurich: all the students were wearing white coats. I can remember Henry Van de Velde [of the Bauhaus School] saying: 'I want to create a laboratory'. They weren't all wearing white coats, but he certainly was. The staff all wore white coats, and you could see that the people who were teaching calligraphy were true craftspeople. In the 1930s, some of these experts in lettering became modernists and then subsequently reverted to being more conservative. I think in Switzerland, there is also a sort of intermittent nationalism that shows itself, when people get a bit worried about being either a bit modernist or being a bit constructivist.

DC: Did anyone from the Swiss scene come to visit you in London?

RH: Yes, Lohse did. I remember it very clearly because there was a painting of mine on the wall and it was a very simple piece with vertical lines in red, white, blue and black: a simple repetition of five lines repeated on the left and right of the work, and he just pointed at one line and said, 'That one should be green!' Right after the war, he was quite a playful designer, but I think he subsequently became much more rigid. So, I suppose the changing values of different generations was of interest to us at the time.

Then there was Emil Ruder, whom I had met in Basel. I think I went to Basel twice. I can remember a moment in Ruder's flat: he was gazing out the window, and he said: 'a hundred years ago, all this was just cows. We are very primitive.' Here is a copy of a letter Ruder sent me (page 125), which he wrote after I had asked him to come to teach in Bristol. We had purchased the complete range of Univers for the department's composing room. It was important because it was a new sans-serif typeface with a variety of sizes, widths and weights and it had only just become available. Ruder understood this type so well; he did a lot of specimens that were featured in *Typografische Monatsblätter*. I thought we needed him here, and he responded and said he would come, but then he got ill, so he wrote me this letter explaining why he couldn't come. In a sense, Ruder saw the work of a designer as essentially being a craftsperson, which, I think, is a whole interesting trend in Switzerland.

Another interesting tendency of the Swiss that initially interested us was the idea of grids, which were unheard of at the time in Britain. When you look at Swiss works you see this extremely rigid gridded layout, whereas back then this is something that, in the UK, we would just have done intuitively or according to tradition – there would have been no standardisation. Well, it's also oddly relevant that Ruder's letter was carefully folded. Looking back, I think this folding definitely inspired me in terms of the work I did later for the Whitechapel Gallery.

Making use of different ways of folding a sheet may have derived from the precise folding of that letter. I now realise it was probably very important.

DC: It seems you were the first to do invitations that folded out into posters for Whitechapel?

RH: I'm not sure, I certainly didn't know whether it had been done before. Still, it just seemed logical because, when I went to work there, they had been sending out posters in rolls, which is more expensive. Consequently, it seemed logical to just fold them up. Then you realised you didn't want to have folding through the type, so the folding would dictate the structure. In a way it wasn't done in the sense of it being a grid – that's what all Müller-Brockmann's stuff was about, in his posters he has things set on a grid. He uses this method to structure the elements, but it's not really done for any practical reason.

It was either on the way to or from Ulm, we were in Zurich, and we peeled a Müller-Brockmann *Tonhalle* poster off a wall because we thought it was so good we wanted to bring it home. It was constructivist in terms of style; it was geometrical because it was organised based on a grid.

Coming back to Whitechapel, the letters were sent out according to their weight. There were all kinds of practical considerations, which were interesting: how heavy the paper was, if you would be sending a lot of things together, it would be priced by Royal Mail in one particular bracket, or it would have to be bumped up into the next bracket...

Here is an Odermatt piece that Ken Garland gave me (page 123). It's dated 1958, and is for Grammo Studio, Zurich – it's so original and so beautifully typeset, so close to the edge. You can see how wonderfully accurate the machining was. Whereas in British printing for instance, there was a tolerance of up to 3 mm. You could be 3 mm off and the customer could not complain! That was just the British standard. Technical training here in Britain just disappeared after the Second World War. Gradually everything deteriorated in terms of standards at many printers; the whole British attitude to technology is very un-Swiss. If there's a mountain, the Swiss will push through it! Strangely enough though, I'm not necessarily an admirer of Swiss politics. I can remember when there was a referendum, the referendum was against joining the United Nations, which to me was completely extraordinary. It's like [Brexit] here, the idea of leaving the European Union. There's a sort of mentality which you need in order to make things work, whereas here, there is a lot of not caring – if you have that with printers, it's just awful. So, I think there's always been a certain admiration for the Swiss desire to get things right, and also their seriousness. *Neue Grafik* is basically a very serious magazine. Many of those designers had a social attitude that was extremely mature and deliberate, which is rare. I don't think we ever had anyone of the calibre of Max Bill or Gerstner for example, people who really thought deeply about things and had a broad worldview, along with political and cultural interests. Take, for instance, the Royal College of Art here: the level of discussion and intensity is very, very low, as compared to Switzerland. Also – it's probably no longer true now because of computers – but the relationship with craftsmanship, calligraphy and lettering in Switzerland certainly remained alive and well through the 1960s. I knew a student of Armin Hofmann's. He would just go on and on and on doing the same curve until it was exactly perfect, as though he were a sculptor, it had to be just right. On the other hand, there was Fritz Bühler, who was a much more commercial artist and teacher, who said that it drove him crazy when students would waste time actually trying to make something perfect. It's all about craft. I remember the work of Hermann Eidenbenz; there's a collection of his workbooks at the Museum für Gestaltung. His work in Germany after the Second World War, much of it in packaging, is astonishing in terms of its traditional craftsmanship, and the precise skill of his calligraphy is amazing, it contrasted with a strictly modernist book on film he did for an exhibition in Basel published in 1947. It was one of the first really gridded works: he broke the type up into phrases as though it was being spoken, he created a sort of dynamic typography. I would definitely rate him a hero in my book: I think he is totally underrated and there should be a book about him. There are books about totally mediocre people – not Swiss designers, are there any mediocre Swiss designers? Of course things have changed because people now become celebrities, so they have to have books published about them which then sell very well.

Karl Gerstner:

Designing
Programmes

Programme as morphology
Programme as logic
Programme as grid
Programme as photography
Programme as literature
Programme as music

Programme as typeface
Programme as typography
Programme as picture
Programme as method

Alec Tiranti Ltd.
London W. 1.

Grammo Studio

Grammo Studio Zürich 1
Bahnhofstrasse 74 Ecke Uraniastrasse
Telephon (051) 23 28 23

Katalog Ausgabe Nummer 1   1958/59

ERLAND   SWITZERLAND

or Sight-Seeing   **The Land for Sight-Seeing**

ecreation   **and Recreation**

Heart of Europe   **in the very Heart of Europe**

EMIL RUDER   SWB ATYPI ICTA

Fachlehrer für Typographie an der Allgemeinen Gewerbeschule Basel
Hardstraße 173
Telephon 061 41 95 35
Basel-Schweiz

2o.1o.64

Herrn Richard Hollis
West of England College of Art
12 Clifton Park
Bristol 8, England

Sehr geehrter Herr Hollis,

wie Sie vielleicht wissen, bin ich vor einem Jahr ausserordentlich
schwer erkrankt, was zwei schwierige Operationen nötig machte. Ich war
dann für 6 Monate arbeitsunfähig.
Heute fühle ich mich wieder sehr wohl, bin von den Aerzten als völlig
geheilt erklärt worden. In Abständen von zwei Monaten muss ich mich
über meinen Gesundheitszustand kontrollieren lassen.
Soeben war ich zur Kontrolle bei meinem Arzt, der mir äusserste Zu-
rückhaltung in meiner Arbeit empfahl.
Und nun das Schlimme: Er verbot mir kategorisch eine Auslandsreise,
solange ich noch nicht besser erholt bin.
Ich stehe nun vor der peinlichen Aufgabe, Sie über meine Unmöglichkeit
noch dieses Jahr nach Bristol zu kommen, zu informieren.
Es tut mir wirklich sehr leid, Ihnen diesen Bericht geben zu müssen.
Persönlich glaubte ich mich für eine solche Reise fähig, umso mehr, da
ich mich sehr wohl fühle. Anderseits kann ich mich über einen ärztlich
Rat nicht hinwegsetzen.
Mein Interesse für Bristol bleibt aber unenetwegt und ich hoffe sehr,
dass ich nächstes Jahr, sofern dies noch gewünscht wird, zu Ihnen
kommen kann.
Ich bitte Sie und Ihre Kollegen sehr um Entschuldigung und hoffe auf
Ihr Verständnis in meiner Lage.

Mit freundlichen Grüssen

Robin Kinross

DEMIAN CONRAD: Could you begin by elaborating on the role that Swiss publications and publishers such as Graphis, *Neue Grafik*, Niggli Verlag and many others played in helping to diffuse the concepts of Swiss graphic design?

ROBIN KINROSS: That is something I have written about and have been observing, so I think my position is partly that of an historian, as well as a bit of a participant. For me, it was always about a sort of magical concept of Switzerland. There was a point when I thought I had a chance to really produce something in Switzerland. I had met Jost Hochuli for the first time at a conference in England. It was in the 1970s, I was a student and Jan Tschichold had just died. Jost was in the process of organising the first really important exhibition on Tschichold's work in Zurich. We talked a little bit and I told him that I knew he was working on this exhibition and I would love to see the catalogue. He was very generous; we shook hands. Then, later in the year, a catalogue arrived – he had remembered. That was the beginning. I didn't see him for years, until 1990, at another conference in England. I came into a room, and Jost said, 'Hello Robin, let's shake hands, ...' he had remembered everything. By then, I had begun publishing books and, as we were chatting, I mentioned that he should get the book *Designing Books* [*Bücher Machen* in German] back into print. So it became a project: he was going to make a German edition for VGS (*Verlagsgemeinschaft*) in St. Gallen, and I was to make an English edition. That was our first project together. The agreement was that the English edition would be produced in Switzerland. For me, it was sort of a dream come true to actually go there and work with a printer in Switzerland and oversee the production, as well as experience a bit of Swiss culture: not just as a tourist but as someone engaged in real production. This first book did well. It's no longer around because we decided that it was actually a book of a certain period, and after some years we realised that you would have to update it and make a new book, not just reprint the same work. I don't know if you know this book? It's a bit lost now. It doesn't tell you how to design books but rather gives you an overview on designing books, with many examples of books from all over, and there is a whole section introducing Jost's work as a proof of what he had been able to do.

DC: That sounds really interesting. So which printer did you use to produce Jost's book?

RK: The printer was Druckerei Ostschweiz in St. Gallen. I think Jost would say he's somewhat provincial, someone from the eastern part of Switzerland. I know that he has felt himself to be a little bit out of it, even as seen from Zurich, although of course he had connections there. He generally does regional publishing jobs with the VGS. Mostly they produce books about St. Gallen, Canton St. Gallen and that region. There are several books about the industries of St. Gallen, lacemaking, agricultural festivals, local customs, and so on. The books are beautifully designed, of course. I don't think they are really known outside the region, but I found them very appealing. It is run by the VGS Cooperative: they would get together in a restaurant every month to make plans for future publications. This sort of Swiss democracy was very interesting to me. I remember once meeting Jost in a café: he was with a group of people from the town and it felt like a real democratic gathering. There was an accountant, a shopkeeper, a graphic designer, a dentist or a doctor and they were all just having coffee together. I thought that this mixture of classes and professions was really nice. I said that I didn't think it could happen as easily in Britain. Jost was surprised, but he agreed that it was more feasible in Switzerland.

DC: Robin, you have acquired a certain perspective from both countries, being British, but also from having experienced working and living in Switzerland. In your view, what are the differences in the approach to design in each of these countries?

RK: I admit to feeling a certain dissatisfaction with my own British culture. Things have changed a lot since I started out as a student in the 1970s. In those days, there was still the question of modernism. Post-modernism was coming, but I think we felt and I can say 'we' because I had some friends that felt – and who still feel – the same way, namely that Great Britain has not truly become a modern country.

DC: Interestingly enough, the philosopher Alain de Botton also made that comment in a Channel 4 documentary about architecture in Britain, saying that it had not changed or become properly modern…

RK: Things were always rather outmoded here, you could see it very clearly in the modern architecture of the 1920s and 1930s. At the time, the pioneers were Germany, France and Switzerland. Britain was always catching up or learning from those other places. We had a solid engi-neering tradition, which you still see in architects like Norman Foster and Richard Rogers. They are closely associated with engineering, which, as you know, is something to be celebrated. This was my position and, as a result, I was drawn towards the whole Swiss culture. I've been talking about Switzerland, but another country I admire is the Netherlands, and it was probably even more important to me. I always had Dutch friends, I speak Dutch and am married to a Dutch woman. I really enjoy being in that country and their modernism was part of it, but it wasn't the whole story. Again, I have to use more or less political language, but I felt it was a more democratic society. Therein lay the attraction. We had our revolution too early. We killed our king in the 1640s, but that proved to be premature, so we brought the monarchy back in 1660. So the British experience was very different from the obvious European example – which is France. France had its revolution in 1789, and this then set the template for Europe. Germany and other countries had their revolutions a bit later, in the 1840s. It became normal to have your revolution then reform. But Britain went down a really exceptional path. We acquired our Empire, and this changed everything. Even now we are still suffering or living through the Empire experience. That is partly what Brexit is about. We don't understand why we can't just be an ordinary European country like France, Germany, Italy, the Netherlands or Portugal. All those countries also had empires, but somehow they were able to lose their empires and then become more or less normal countries. So it's a deep history with which to contend.

DC: There was this important moment in Switzerland, where designers like Armin Hoffmann, Emil Ruder, Josef Müller-Brockmann, Hans-Rudolf Bosshard and many others were writing books and providing methodologies around how to approach typography and design. How did that affect Britain back then? How was that perceived?

RK: Well I think my interest in Swiss work did not centre, as was typical, around Müller-Brockmann. For me the interesting people were Karl Gerstner and then Bruno Monguzzi, whom I thought were doing something rather different from the stereotype of Swiss typography. For a couple of years, I taught one day a week at Ravensbourne College, south of London. The building was constructed in the 1960s, and the whole school felt like a tribute to modernism. I encountered teachers who had fallen under the spell of Müller-Brockmann. I remember that the library held at least ten copies of his work *The Graphic Designer and his Design Problems* (*Gestaltungsprobleme des Grafikers*). Of course, this was in the 1980s and, by then, the library also held many other books, but I was told that, in the beginning, there was only Müller-Brockmann. That was it. It was at Ravensbourne that I met Simon Johnston, who made his mark as one of the key figures in publishing *Octavo* magazine, along with Mark Holt and Hamish Muir, who were also teaching at the school. They were part of the younger generation who had followed in the wake of Wolfgang Weingart: he was really their model. They were also interested in the history of these developments. What was extraordinary was that their magazine was so well printed, and, astonishingly, it was printed in England. They had been able to attain Swiss standards of production in England and I'm still not sure how they managed it. I remember it clearly: people were astonished at the production quality of this magazine. I didn't truly experience the Müller-Brockmann phenomenon at the outset; for me in the 1970s it was already old news. Nevertheless, I can understand that, for the people who were working in the 1950s, or even the 1960s, it must have been like a breath of fresh air, something major. You would have to ask people like Richard Hollis; I know Richard is coming to speak with you. He can describe it better than I can. Actually, for me personally, the truly important person was English: Anthony Froshaug (page 135). He had been teaching at Ulm and he had experienced the Swiss phenomenon there, but his work was always more complicated than so-called Swiss typography. In some respects it was more like Gerstner's work. There was always something more complicated going on. I saw things very much through

Anthony's eyes in those days. Richard [Hollis] had absorbed the lessons of Froshaug much earlier. British designers of that generation travelled to Switzerland by train on a Grand Tour of sorts: they might go first to Paris, then perhaps to Munich, then on to Basel. Anthony did this: he went to Zurich to visit Max Bill, then he went on to Italy and ended up in Venice. In the book I did on Anthony, the meeting with Bill is documented in their letters. This was in 1953. Froshaug showed his work to Bill, who wrote him a severe letter to the effect of 'your work shows mistakes and it is not as we would do it' and 'this is not good enough and therefore I cannot have you as a teacher at Ulm'. Nevertheless, in my opinion, Bill was a wonderful designer, I mean really wonderful. Sure, he was dogmatic, but he always remained inventive. You can see this quite clearly through the fact that he also explored painting and 3D work, as well as architecture and graphic design. I suppose back then, you could still do all those things without inhibition, before all this specialisation took over. There is a story: it was 1980 and I was still at the University of Reading, I had just graduated. One of the students was Swiss. His name was Kaspar Mühlemann; I think he was from the eastern part of Switzerland. Kaspar belonged to a family of printers: his father had a printing business. He had been sent to the UK by his father so he could improve his English. He gave me this book (page 134) written by Bosshard, *Technische Grundlagen zur Satzherstellung*, and published by Verlag des Bildungsverbandes Schweizerischer Typographen in Zurich. I guess he knew I could read German, he knew I would be interested, and for me it remains a wonderful book that is probably out of print. Certainly in those days Swiss printers and compositors received serious training, and graphic design was integrated as much as possible into printing. Again this was another ideal of Swiss culture, that the people making the end product were also educated about design, and that there was a sort of integration. A book like this is the product of that idea. I find it slightly crazy, it's a bit extreme, but it's also very inspiring just to think this is what you could learn. It is from the era of the old technology: it's about metal and photo-setting, just before the rise of the personal computer. There are some crazy things included, such as the formats of newspapers of the world. If you want to know the regulation sizes of the *New York Times* or *Die Welt* or *Paris Match*, you can find out there. When I started out, I met some of the people who had trained as type compositors or *Schriftsetzers*. They were generally nice and also interesting, mostly men, and you could tell they had really had a thorough education. Bosshard is one of those; he is still active in

Zurich. As you were saying, I don't think he designs anything now, but he is still actively writing. He also did more or less conceptual art and he made artists' books as well. His son Markus did a lot of drawings for this book. I think they were, as a matter of course, done by hand. I really don't know how useful they were or if anyone ever used these books. Nonetheless, there is the sheer pleasure of discovering the information they contain; in that sense, the book is inspiring. I expect you will meet with some of the younger British designers now. You might say that, in this country, they are recreating reproductions of Müller-Brockmann. There were some British designers in the 1960s who emulated that work and now there are imitations of that. However, I'm not a student of this design work. For me, if the content is interesting, then that's enough. You know, you don't have to do much. If you have a beautiful photograph, you just place it, and the photograph is the focus, that's all you need. You have to print it properly, on good paper. I think there's an overproduction of material and we are completely saturated with images, books, and magazines – there is too much of all that. After so much design, I've had enough!

DC: I have this conviction that the International Style should be truly international. It should function as a kind of global way to communicate between countries. Nowadays it also seems that there is a return to a kinder, gentler, more national graphic design. Do you think this is really a thing, or just a subjective impression?

RK: I don't know the answer to that. I think there was an International Style that you could perceive in architecture. If you look around London for instance, especially in the case of public housing from the 1970s, it seems very much to be inspired by the International Style of the 1930s. I could take you to housing that bears an astonishing resemblance to the work of Dutch architect Jacobus Johannes Pieter Oud, or the Swiss housing of the 1930s from the Swiss Werkbund in Neubühl. You see it here in the UK, in buildings built in the 1970s and 1980s. It was somewhat the same with graphic design. There was an International Style; Richard Hollis has talked about it. It was about a way of doing it, not really style design, but rather it produced things that were ordinary and sensible, and that worked. In terms of architecture it was good for public housing because you don't necessarily want an amazing building on every street; you might just want a street that looks calm and comfortable and that's it. You don't want to be astonished every moment, sometimes you just want something pleasant and easy on the eye. I think that was part of the essence of the International Style. That was the idea. It's the opposite of Frank Gehry or Daniel Libeskind, star architects who go around creating astonishing buildings. I don't know how much you know of English, British architecture? There's a practice here, Caruso St. John Architects, they're a bit like Herzog & De Meuron, however I think they are even more about doing something quiet that you don't notice. Just ordinary. I think in a way, that really was the modern dream. At least, in my understanding. However, somehow it went wrong: when people talk about modernist architecture now, they tend to mean amazing architecture or signature architecture, where you recognise the designer because you know they always do similar things and the building always has a certain look. There is a whole other British culture that has nothing to do with modernism and has also been revived. This is a sort of gentle classicism, which you can see in the architecture of brick buildings. The Prince of Wales for example has been a focus for all this. And we go back to politics: Britain still has a monarchy and an aristocracy that influence our daily life. This nostalgic classicism has sometimes been reflected in British graphic design too. It is so different from the democratic spirit of Switzerland!

Hans Rudolf Bosshard

Technische Grundlagen
zur Satzherstellung

Retrospective Exhibition   *Anthony Froshaug*   **Typography 1945/1965**

9.30 am to 8.30 pm Mondays to Fridays   from 26 April 1965
9.30 am to 12 noon Saturdays
Watford College of Technology Hempstead Road Watford Herts

Sara De Bondt

DEMIAN CONRAD: Hi Sara, tell us a bit about how you became interested in publishing and about the object you have brought here today.

SARA DE BONDT: I run a small publishing house with Antony Hudek called Occasional Papers. The first book we published was *The Master Builder: Talking with Ken Briggs* (page 144–145), an interview with English designer Ken Briggs, which I did with my friend, graphic designer Fraser Muggeridge. In 2008, my partner Antony, who is an art historian, and I were talking about starting a publishing company: it felt like a logical thing to do together. One day Fraser told me about a fantastic exhibition on the work of someone named Ken Briggs at the Pump House Gallery. I responded, 'Who is that guy? I've never heard of him'. The only information available on him was Richard Hollis's piece in *Eye* magazine on Briggs's designs for the National Theatre. The gallery was a tiny space in South London. Antony and I decided this was an excellent pretext to publish something to get the word out about the exhibition and Ken – and that was the start of Occasional Papers (OP). Fraser and I went to interview Ken in his studio. Pump House Gallery and the National Theatre, who own a lot of Briggs's work, each pitched in £300 and OP covered the other expenses. Within two weeks, we had interviewed Ken, transcribed, edited, designed and printed the book, and, at the closing of the exhibition, we held a book launch. The publication was not much longer than a brochure, but it was our first publishing project and we learned a lot from it. I discovered some of the connections between different generations of designers and international contacts, and the influence of magazines. When I asked Ken how he had come to discover Swiss graphic design, he told me that Germano Facetti, who had been designing for Penguin Books, had shown him a magazine called *Neue Grafik*, referring to it as 'the future of design'. All of them were really into it. Ken was among the first to bring Swiss design into the mainstream in London. His style was really simple, with a heavy dose of Helvetica. Wim Crouwel used to call Ken 'The Colourist' because of his abundant use of colour. Ken didn't like to use black, he preferred overprinting two colours to make black as a costsaving measure. It was funny talking to him. For example, in his heyday, he would sometimes design a poster that the client would only see and comment on after it was printed. It's such a different way of dealing with design than nowadays.

DC: How was Swiss design perceived when you were studying graphic design?

SDB: Swiss design was not around so much. American grunge designers such as David Carson were popular back then, and I was really into the work of the collective Grapus, who were French. In Belgium, we received the influence of Swiss style second hand via the Dutch designers, through the work of the likes of Total Design, and later on Experimental Jetset, Mevis & Van Deursen or Irma Boom. My teaching was more centred around illustration and fine art rather than any history of graphic design. After graduation, I continued my studies at the Jan van Eyck Akademie in the Netherlands. The students there came from all over the world. We all went on a trip to London, and a friend of mine from Brazil remarked, 'Oh, look at that, they only use Helvetica in London, it's crazy!' It was so true! Marks & Spencer's, along with several main brands, were using Helvetica and it was everywhere. There was a sort of fetish for Swiss design in London. You must talk to Tony Brook from Spin, I've been told he has a vast collection of Swiss design and a lot of the Unit Editions books are in that style. The UK branch is also very active in the Swissbased AGI (Alliance Graphique Internationale).

DC: Why do you think the Swiss style became so successful in the UK?

SDB: I think there was a moment in the early 2000s when designers were reacting against postmodernism and returning to a more strippeddown version of design. When I used to work for Daniel Eatock at Foundation 33, for example, he was obsessed with

Akzidenz-Grotesk. However, there is also a creepy side to that modernism, one which many younger designers are questioning today, related to capitalism. That fake neutral, clean look makes you look stable, efficient, affordable, accessible. The UK is more market-oriented than Belgium in that respect.

DC: There is always a to and fro of ideology, and its effect upon approaches to design. What's interesting in my opinion is that England is an island. You could also say that, in a sense, Switzerland is also a sort of island: it's neutral, excluded from Europe, it's set in the middle of the Alps, so there is a mental and somewhat physical sense of being insular. We tend towards not being particularly inclusive, and that is something we seem to share with the British. For instance, when I was a student, I remember a colleague of mine, Edoardo Cecchin, who showed me a beautiful black-and-white book by photographer Albert Watson, designed by David Carson, entitled *Cyclops*. It is a brilliant bit of production, printed in Agfa Cristalraster, with four shades of grey. I remember that our teacher at the time, Bruno Monguzzi, criticised it strongly. He said it was just a waste of energy and time and was not a rational solution. I do not know if that might be qualified as a sort of Swiss perfectionism or protectionism.

SDB: It's true, some influential Swiss designers have lived in London, such as Laurenz Brunner, Corinne Gisel, Nicole Udry and Cornell Windlin. Others shuttle between the two countries, like Matthias Clottu and Jonathan Hares. However, that is the case for designers of all nationalities. Before the increased school fees, London really was a kind of magnet.

DC: Do you think all those designers in turn brought a little something British back to Switzerland?

SDB: Yes, I do think so, perhaps a touch of anarchy, I don't know, you should tell me.

DC: I know that Windlin did spend some time working with Brody, and then he went on to design some typefaces for the Fuse Project. Notably the *Hello World!* poster for the Museum für Gestaltung, which was considered quite un-Swiss at the time. You had mentioned the dialogue between the generations. I think the manner in which know-ledge is transferred to younger generations is so important. If we can take only one important lesson from Müller-Brockmann, it should be that design is not about style, but methodology. Unfortunately not everybody gets that, and some studios just see it as a kind of marketing tool to improve sales. I also think it's interesting how much things have changed because of easier access to travel. You mentioned Hares, who is currently doing books in London, but living and teaching in Lausanne. That would have been impossible before the era of cheap shuttle flights. With those, you could come here for a few days, do some deals and meetings and then go home, that was quite unique.

I get the impression that London is quite inclusive. If you have something interesting to say, you can say it. In Switzerland I feel it's a bit more conservative. As for me, by birth I'm a Catholic, but I'm slowly becoming more Calvinist. Here in the French area where I'm from, it's Calvinist and you feel a lot of pressure to work hard, keep quiet, not talk to strangers, keep the front of your house spotless, stay within the lines, and mind your own business... I feel that this culture could easily generate the sort of attitude you see with Müller-Brockmann. He was considered a radical at the time, but it was not in a noisy way, he was not shouting from the rooftops. Rather it was a lower-case, discreet sort of radicalism, rhythmic, and beautifully crafted, like his famous music poster for the Tonhalle, which made use of Abstract Concrete inspired illustration and typography that was never overly chaotic or noisy – you always felt there was a system behind it all. Max Huber, for instance, is the opposite. As a Swiss designer in Italy, he was in a completely different cultural context. He used a lot of colours, and many overlapping layers. Having been raised in Ticino, I was exposed to both styles, the more playful and Mediterranean style of Italy, notably the Milan designers, as well as the more Calvinist and sober influences from Zurich and Basel.

SDB: It's interesting that you refer to religion. Do you think that's still exerting an influence today? Perhaps you are right: Protestant countries such as the Netherlands, England or Switzerland used to be better known for their typographic skills. Catholic ones such as France or Belgium have received more recognition for their comics and illustration. Still, don't you think the lines are more blurred now? Anyway, what about the rest of the world? We should stop being so focused on Western Europe.

DC: I remember that, at one time, the British studio Tomato was using a lot of studio images. Now it seems like it's all about typography, would you agree?

SDB: **Perhaps it has to do with speed. Designers nowadays are under so much pressure to make something fast for next to no money. Creating an image or illustration is more timeconsuming than using an interesting typeface.**

Maybe you should interview someone who knows about Jan Tschichold, since he lived in England, then went to Germany and then on to Switzerland and, in the process, his way of thinking changed. I wonder how much his new environments influenced his radical shift in ideas.

DC: Yes, you are right, he did make a big shift. His newer typographic approach verged on the dogmatic. One might even say that his shift towards a more traditional approach was radical in itself. During a certain period, from the advent of postmodernism to the 2010s, Switzerland became increasingly disconnected from its modernist heritage. For the Swiss, it was seen as a sort of rejection of their image of being uptight or focused only on essentials. Certainly, we did have some great postmodern designers, such as Rosmarie Tissi, Siegfried Odermatt and Hans-Rudolf Lutz. Recently there has been a certain revivalism, new generations seem to be exploring their roots, and academics have become interested and have begun to research the field of Swiss design, as we can see with Louise Paradis's brilliant student research project *Thirty Years of Swiss Typographic Discourse in the Typografische Monatsblätter (TM RSI SGM 1960–1990)*.

SDB: **I think it's excellent that graphic designers are becoming more aware of what has gone before and that more publishers are into the history of graphic design. Nevertheless, let's not forget about the future and not be too nostalgic either. The people who came before us were also responsible for many negative things we are dealing with today, such as the climate crisis and the legacy of colonisation.**

DC: Do you think Brexit is going to affect graphic design? Do you think that London might possibly lose its creative edge?

SDB: I'm sure it will have an effect. Back in 2002, it was easy for me to move to England, set up my studio, and start a company as an EU citizen. I know people who have already changed their plans to move here or have moved away because of Brexit. The economic consequences are surely going to worsen. It will affect teaching too: many people I know who teach are worried. If Britain leaves the EU, all EU students in Britain will have to start paying tuition fees, amounting to around £9,000 per year. When I was teaching at the Royal College, half of the students were from the EU – Portugal, France, Switzerland, or Germany. If they stop coming, they will end up with primarily wealthy students. That will undoubtedly have a trickle-down effect on the quality of teaching, graduates and the whole design economy.

Book Design in Switzerland

The Master Builder
Talking with Ken Briggs

Sara De Bondt and Fraser Muggeridge

J.Mül

Gesta
Grafik
The G
Desig
Les p
graph

I was very keen on doing drop-out photographs and printing double blacks, with blue underneath everything first. And I didn't mind red, but Ken particularly liked red, orange and black, so sometimes I would try to please him. They called me the colourist. When I was introduced to the Dutch designer Wim Crouwel[10] he said 'Ken, I'm pleased to finally meet the colourist.'

Apart from the full-colour advertising, the programmes were printed in two colours. Why was that?

In those days most machines could only print in two colours, and we couldn't afford full-colour throughout. The printers bought a two-colour Heidelberg lithographic press and wanted to use it. Sometimes we'd try out flat gold or silver as a full-page background to see how it worked.

Did you go to the printers?

Yes. I like printers, unlike a lot of designers. I love going there. I like the smell, the activity and the noise, seeing it 'hot off the press'. I used to go every week or so to oversee the printing.

What was your working environment like?

By the end of the 1960s the National had become so successful that you couldn't get in, you couldn't book. It was a very vibrant and exciting time, all the plays I saw during that period were absolutely brilliant. Everyone was mucking in, helping each other. Eventually, Olivier wanted all of us to work from there so I was given a tiny office in a prefab hut in Aquinas Street. I'd go there, and people would come in and chat all morning. It was like a social club. After work at home I thought 'I haven't done anything, and I have this bloody programme to do.' So I would find myself designing through the night again.

In the later posters you start to use diagonal typography. How did this come about?

Eventually bums on seats dropped off, and the National decided they needed a new approach and wanted to advertise on the underground. I tried to find out more details: which station,

Booking leaflets, 1969–70

14

15

147

Information for Navigating
These Complicated Topics

Index of Names

List of Objects

Page 50
Bruno Maag:
File

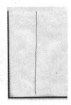

Page 51
Bruno Maag:
Hand-drawn
line

Page 52
Bruno Maag:
Helvetica
typeface

Page 53
Bruno Maag:
Univers
typeface

Page 68
Fraser
Muggeridge:
Book cover,
*Das Grosse
Drei-Farben-
Mischbuch*

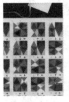

Page 69
Fraser
Muggeridge:
Book,
*Das Grosse
Drei-Farben-
Mischbuch*

Page 70
Fraser
Muggeridge:
Binding,
*Das Grosse
Drei-Farben-
Mischbuch*

Page 82
Freda Sack:
ISTD
newsletter,
detail

Page 83
Freda Sack:
Book signed
by JMB

Page 84
Freda Sack:
Invitation to
ISTD lecture

Page 85
Freda Sack:
ISTD lecture,
article

Page 96
Holger Jacobs:
Kami puppet

Page 97
Holger Jacobs:
Schauspielhaus
Catalogue, ill.

Page 98
Holger Jacobs:
Schauspielhaus
Catalogue, ill.

Page 99
Holger Jacobs:
Schauspielhaus
Catalogue, cover

Page 110
Michele
Jannuzzi:
Book,
Max Huber

Page 111
Michele
Jannuzzi:
Book,
Max Huber

Page 122
Richard Hollis:
Book,
*Designing
Programmes*

Page 123
Richard Hollis:
Booklet,
Grammo Studio

Page 124
Richard Hollis:
Booklet,
Swiss Tourism

Page 125
Richard Hollis:
Letter from
Emil Ruder

Page 134
Robin Kinross:
Book cover,
*Technische
Grundlagen zur
Satzherstellung*

Page 135
Robin Kinross:
Book detail,
*Technische
Grundlagen zur
Satzherstellung*

Page 144
Sara De Bondt:
Booklet,
*The Master
Builder: Talking
with Ken Briggs*

Page 145
Sara De Bondt:
Booklet,
*The Master
Builder: Talking
with Ken Briggs*

Page 87
Holger Jacobs:
Oops!

Page 14
Demian Conrad:
Research wall

Page 14
Demian Conrad:
Flyer

Page 15
Demian Conrad:
Installation
setting

Page 15
Demian Conrad:
Discussion

Contributor's Biographies (in order of appearance)

David Kilian Beck (1982)
Head of the Culture Department at the Embassy of Switzerland in the United Kingdom. With a background in education, he holds a Master's degree in Photographic Studies from the University of Westminster and worked in different capacities in the cultural sector before assuming his post at the Embassy. He has been a trustee of the Swiss Cultural Fund UK since 2011 and was the project-lead of Ambit, a series of design exhibitions.

Demian Conrad (1974)
is a Swiss graphic designer, creative director and researcher based in Biel/Bienne. He has authored several books on design. In 2007 he founded Automatico Studio, a multi-disciplinary consultancy firm. He has been a professor at HEAD, Geneva since 2016, and has been a member of the Alliance Graphique Internationale (AGI) since 2017.

Adrian Shaughnessy (1953)
is a British graphic designer, writer, lecturer, editor and publisher. From 1988 until 2004 he was creative director and co-founder of the design studio Intro. In 2010 he co-founded the design publishing company Unit Editions. He is a writer for *Eye* magazine, *Design Observer* and *The Guardian*, as well as a visiting tutor at the Royal College of Art.

Bruno Maag (1962)
is a British/Swiss type designer and co-founder of the type design company Dalton Maag, and a public speaker who lectures internationally.

Fraser Muggeridge (1973)
is a British graphic and type designer based in London, and founder of Fraser Muggeridge studio, and the Typography Summer School in London and New York. Muggeridge has been a visiting lecturer at the University of Reading since 2003.

Freda Sack (1951–2019)
was a British type designer based in London. In 1990, Sack co-founded the type design company The Foundry with partner David Quay. She worked extensively in design education, lecturing and mentoring, and was a longstanding Director and Board Member of the International Society of Typographic Designers (ISTD).

Holger Jacobs (1967)
is a German graphic designer based in London who founded the studio
Mind Design in 1999. He is a professor of typography at the University
of Applied Science in Düsseldorf, a member of the Chartered Society
of Designers (CSD), the International Society of Typographic Designers
(ISTD) and the Royal College of Art Society.

Michele Jannuzzi (1967)
is a British/Swiss graphic designer based in London and Lugano who
co-founded the studio Jannuzzi Smith in 1993. He has been a visiting
lecturer at many universities, including the Central Saint Martins College
of Art and Design in London, Università della Svizzera Italiana (USI) in
Lugano and IE University in Madrid. Jannuzzi is also the author of several
texts on the subject of design and communication.

Richard Hollis (1934)
is a former freelance British graphic designer. He has worked as a printer,
art editor, production manager, teacher and lecturer. After working in Paris
in the early 1960s, he co-founded the School of Design in Bristol with
Norman Potter. His books include *Schweizer Grafik 1920–1965; Henry
van de Velde: The Artist as Designer* and *Graphic Design in the Twentieth
Century*. Hollis was appointed a Royal Designer for Industry in 2005.
See *Richard Hollis Designs for the Whitechapel* by Christopher Wilson.

Robin Kinross (1949)
is a British typographer and editor based in London. In 1980 he founded
the publishing house Hyphen Press, producing literature and books
on typography and graphic design. Among his writings are the books
Modern Typography and *Unjustified Texts.*

Sara De Bondt (1977)
is a Belgian graphic designer who lived in London from 2002 until 2015,
running her design studio and teaching at Central Saint Martins and
the Royal College of Art. In 2008 she co-founded Occasional Papers
with Antony Hudek. She is currently a PhD student at KASK School of
Art/Ghent University. Sara has been a member of Alliance Graphique
Internationale (AGI) since 2017.

Acknowledgments

I would like to express my deep gratitude for my friends, all the people with whom I collaborated, and the institutions that supported this long-term project. I would also like to express my heartfelt thanks to: Layla Benitez-James, Daniel Blattler, Hans Rudolf Bosshard, Markus Sebastian Braun, Jonathan Brantschen, Roland Brauchli, Erich Brechbühl, Arnaud Chemin, Alessia Contin, Richard Doust, Barbara Junod, Mischa Mauch, Jlaria Moscufo, Jens Müller, Lars Müller, Sabina Mueller, NORM (Dimitri Bruni and Manuel Krebs), Giovanna Lisignoli, Pola Rapatt, Bettina Richter, Sabrina Stolfa, Rosmarie Tissi, Stuart Tolley and Cornel Windlin, for their ongoing stimulation, encouragement and contribution.

Colophon

Editorial Concept
Demian Conrad

Texts
Adrian Shaughnessy
David Kilian Beck
Demian Conrad

Transcriptions
Jenny Benyon
Clare Gaunt
Edward Maltby
Simon A. Thomas
Louise Thomas

Editing
Aviva Cashmira Kakar
Demian Conrad

Translation
Aviva Cashmira Kakar

Corrector
Friederike Christoph

Book Design
Automatico Studio
Demian Conrad

Design Assistants
Miles Bögli
Jasmina Molano
Dario Pianesi
Maïra Zimmermann

Paper
Sirio Color Black 290 gsm
Munken Print White
80 gsm bulk 1.5

Typeface used
Univers Next Medium

ISBN 978-3-7212-1007-1
2022 Niggli, ein Imprint der
Braun Publishing AG, Salenstein
www.niggli.ch

Special thanks to:

Embassy of Switerland
in the United Kingdom
swiss cultural fund UK
Pro Helvetia

Schweizerische Eidgenossenschaft
Confédération suisse
Confederazione Svizzera
Confederaziun svizra

Embassy of Switzerland in the United Kingdom

SWISS
cultural
fund UK

swiss arts council
prohelvetia